'988

N

● University of St. Francis
720.284 M684
Mitooka, Eiji,
Airbrushing in rendering /

3 0301 00082319 1

D1404680

AIRBRUSHING
in RENDERING
EIJI MITOOKA & DON DESIGN ASSOCIATES

VNR Van Nostrand Reinhold Company
New York

LIBRARY
College of St. Francis
JOLIET, ILLINOIS

Copyright (c) 1982 by Graphic-sha Co., Ltd.
Library of Congress Catalog Card Number 84-13098
ISBN 0-442-26082-2

All rights reserved. No part of this work covered by the copyright hereon may
be reproduced or used in any form or by any means--graphic, electronic, or
mechanical, including photocopying, recording, taping, or information storage
and retrieval systems--without written permission of the publisher.

Printed in Japan

Published by Van Nostrand Reinhold Company Inc.
135 West 50th Street
New York, New York 10020

Van Nostrand Reinhold Company Limited
Molly Millars Lane
Wokingham, Berkshire RG11 2PY, England

Van Nostrand Reinhold
480 La Trobe Street
Melbourne, Victoria 3000, Australia

Macmillan of Canada
Division of Gage Publishing Limited
164 Commander Boulevard
Agincourt, Ontario M1S 3C7, Canada

16 15 14 13 12 11 10 9 8 7 6 5 4 3 2 1

Library of Congress Cataloging in Publication Data

Mitooka, Eiji.
  Airbrush in rendering.

  Bibliography: p.
  Includes index.
  1.Architectural rendering. 2.Airbrush art--
Technique. I. Title.
NA2780.M58 1985   720'.28'4   84-13098
ISBN 0-442-26082-2

120.284
M684

TABLE OF CONTENTS

128,101

はじめに

私とエアブラシ

　私がエアブラシに関する本を著すとは、我ながらおこがましい仕業と赤面の思いがする。エアブラシと言えば、一般に塗装や写真修整、精密機械類のレンダリングやスーパー・リアリズムのアートに欠かせぬ道具として知られている。関係図書も「エアーブラシ・イラストレーション・テクニック」（誠文堂新光社刊）をはじめとして、鑑賞用・実用向けを問わず行き届いた内容の類書が多く、私もつい先頃までこれらの本を楽しく、素朴な感動をもって眺める読者の一人だったからである。このことからも察せられるとおり、私とエアブラシの付き合いはたかだか三年に過ぎない。正直に言うと、パースを始めて間もない人に筆で広い面積をムラなく塗る技を教えるよりは、エアブラシの使い方を習ってもらう方が手っ取り早いというのがその下心であった。これよりずっと以前、建築関係以外の各種イラストレーションにこの道具を応用してみたのが、私にとってそもそもの馴初めなのだが、もとより筆塗りの補助・修整のつもりで始めたため、クモの糸さながらの細い線を吹き上げるような名人芸は、今もって望むべくもない。

　エアブラシに関してはこのように誠に頼りない経歴しかもたない私が、敢えて本書を梓にのぼせる意図は、誇れるエアブラシング技術があるから、ではもちろんない。ひたすら必要に迫られて、試行錯誤のうちに偶然知ったエアブラシの「ちょっといい経験」を、未だためらっている方々に耳打ちしたいがためである。だから正確には、エアブラシの個性に魅せられて、いわば積極的な目的意識からこれを推すと言うよりは、あくまでもパースを生かす有効な方便として、経験からこれを勧めると言った方がよい。従って、私が必要と感じるエアブラシング技術はプロの必須技量の半分にも満たないことだろう。しかし、レンダラーの自己研鑽のエネルギーは、他の専門技術や感性に一層の磨きをかけることに向けるのが当然である、と私は思う。肩の力を抜いて、エアブラシはそれぐらい手軽で憶するにあたらぬ道具と呑んでかかれば、手探りのうちに思いがけない可能性と発見に出会うことがあるだろう。ちょうど三年前の私のように。

　今日エアブラシのパース部門への進出が著しいが、その利用実態はあまり喧伝されていない。種々のパースの本の頁を無造作に繰ってみる。目を凝らせば、どこか一部にでもエアブラシが使われ、しかもそれが凡庸でない効果を与えている作品に気付くだろう。このようにエアブラシは、特に印刷上の要請もあって国内外のパースに広く利用されてはいるものの、それを看板にしたり、自己のスタイルとして大袈裟に打ち出しているレンダラーが殆どいないために、パースとの相性の良さが表立って来ない。見方を変えれば、レンダラーはブラシング効果の有無、絵の性格、制作条件などを全て睨み合わせた上で、随時この技法の採否を判断しているのであり、さほどにエアブラシの利用範囲が広域にして柔軟であるとも言える。ブラシングの粋は線に在り、と断言するその道のプロもおられるが、私は、エアブラシは本来面のために、面を楽に均一に塗るためにあるものと思っている。建築パースを志す人が修練を積んでいかほどの微細な線を吹き上げる術を学んでも、そうした線の単純な合算が即優れたパースになるわけでないことは、デザイン概論をかじった人に限らず一般の人々にも自明の理である。エアブラシの第一人者と目される方によると、きちんとした指導要綱があれば誰でも三ヶ月で一応の技術は習得できるらしい。それならば、たとえ独習にせよそれだけの期間に基本をしっかりとマスターし、然る後に、パースにおけるその融通無碍の使いわけのコツを身につける方が賢明と言うものである。

　エアブラシは高価な器具である。大型コンプレッサーを備えると、価格の圧力だけでなく、ただでさえ狭苦しい仕事場に悠然と鎮座するその迫力に、私としてはとんでもない食客を背負い込んだような気になる。確かに世話が焼ける。何が気に障ったか急に口もきいてくれない。だが道具を使い馴らすのも仕事と思えば、こんな頼もしい友もないだろう。

エアブラシの「裏表」

エアブラシは、今日のイラストレーションの花形と言ってもよいほど精妙にして技巧的なメディアであるが、その歴史を突きつめると人類の創成期にまで遡るらしい。今から3,500年ほど前（欧州における後期旧石器時代）のオーリニャック人が獣の骨を使って壁に色を吹いている姿を描いた絵は、エアブラシの本に必ずと言ってよいほど挿入されているし、ラスコーの洞窟には、実際にこのようにして吹きつけられたと思われる「手」の輪郭が残されている。日本でも古くから「吹き墨」とか「ふりかけ」とか呼ばれる一種のボカシ技法が焼物や絵画に応用されていたが、現在のエアブラシの原型と呼ぶべき道具は、西欧の産業革命から約50年余の後、そのまだ熱い余波に乗って世に出て来たのである。

エアブラシの発明が正確にいつのことなのか、今もって定かでない。一般に「英国人」チャールズ・L・バーディックがこの道具のパテントを取り、ロンドンに会社を構えた1893年をもってエアブラシの誕生の年としているが、彼は実は米国人であり、米国でエアブラシを発明した後すぐさま英国に渡ってパテントを取り、前述の会社「ファウンテン・ブラッシ・カンパニー」を設立したらしい。ところが、エアブラシ・ケースのデザインを対象にしたと思われる米国のパテントが1888年に登録されており、そのあたりの事情を慮るといよいよ真相は藪の中に隠れてしまう。ともあれ、今日のエアブラシのモデルの多くは1920年頃までに市場に出まわり、専ら写真修整用に大いに重宝がられていたのである。

ところで、事実上の発明者とされるバーディックは極めて多芸多才の士であり、自作の道具を巧みに使って芸術の世界への紹介・普及に努めた。手ずから描いた絵が「メカニスティックである」という理由でロイヤル・アカデミーから受け入れを拒否されたことに一段と奮起した彼は、1900年自らエアブラシ・アートのコンペティションを主催する。この催しの成否は、残念ながら私には不明だが、その後エアブラシがバウハウスの芸術家たちに好んで用いられ、「エスクァイアー」誌の表紙を飾り、現在の隆盛を迎えるに至ったことを思うと、彼の慧眼を讃え、宿願の成就に拍手を送るべきだろう。

今日あちこちで見かける目もあやなポスター一類は、鮮明でリアルな質感を前面に押し出したいわば「表芸」としてのエアブラシであり、これこそ発明者の衣鉢を継ぐ本道なのかもしれない。しかし他方で、アトリエではなく工場といった趣の場所で、一般には馴染みのない分野のために、作家ではなく職人さんの手によって操られるエアブラシがあるのだが、私にはむしろこうした地味な、芸術の陰にある「裏芸」の方がシミジミ慕わしく、また急速な工業化の煤煙を浴びて成長して来たこの用具本来のイメージにしっくりするような気もする。第一私の仕事ぶりが、どう考えてもこの「裏芸」に近い。

レンダリング自体、「アートの制作にイソシム」といった優雅な気分とは程遠い、気骨の折れる制約の多い作業なのだが、背中を丸めてカッティングしたり、マスクで顔面を覆い流し台の横でブラシングする己が姿を改めて思い浮かべてみると、いよいよもって「町工場で塗装作業にイソシム」という風情が濃厚になる。画家が作業台（と呼ぶのか？）の上に這いつくばって筆を動かすところは、昔映画で見た、聖堂の天井壁画を描くミケランジェロの苦しげな仰向けの姿勢とそれをものともしない情熱をホーフツとさせる図であり、私としてはどことなく崇高な感じを抱いてしまう。それに引き比べてみると、私のエアブラシングはいかにも「日々のナリワイ」風であり、あまりにもインダストリアルなのだ。

しかし考えてみれば、レンダラーのエアブラシングは「殆んど塗装」なのである。アーティストやアーティザンの「描く」行為や技とは、ある意味で似而非なる性質をもち、またこの隔たりを無理に埋める必要もない。実のところ、この「塗装面」が我々の技である透視図と手描きの線を引き立たせる見事な裏方ぶりを発揮してくれるのであり、同時に、この家内工業的お手軽さが、誰にでも描ける魅力あるパースへの可能性を拓いてくれるのだと思う。

何故エアブラシか

エアブラシには、グラデーションや色調の変化が自在、色混ぜが簡単、応用の範囲が広いなどの様々な利点がある。加えて、写真を越えるハイパー・リアリスティックな表現力を評価されて発展した用具だけに、パースにとっても格好の手段であることは間違いない。ただ、この道具で画面全体を塗り込めたパースを一人で描けと言われても、私はおそらく御辞退するだろう。実際私の場合、パートナーたちの協力があるおかげで、どこかにエアブラシングの跡を感じさせるパースを描き上げることが出来るのである。

エアブラシそのものは教則本を頼りに回を重ねれば誰でも一通りは扱えるが、パースに応用する際に最も厄介で気が滅入る段階はカッティングなのである。いわゆるエアブラシ・アートでは、漠然とした境界線のないグラデーションにこそ妙味があるとも言えるので、必要不可欠な部分だけ密着マスキングし、後はフリーハンドでカバーできる。このためにはエアブラシを自在に操り、表現の微調整まで出来る技量が必要だが、精密なカッティングと貼り戻しの繁雑な手間仕事の量はずっと少なくて済むだろう。特に図面を基に描くパースでは、対象たる建物は全て明瞭な線で組みたてられている。曖昧なグラデーションの乱用で輪郭線をぼかすことは出来ない。マスキングフィルムを正確に切り離し、再び1ミリのズレもなく元の位置に戻す作業は、いささかマニアックな神経を要するし、更に辛いことに、その巧拙や緻密さの度合いが出来上がりを大いに左右するのである。

では、何故わざわざエアブラシを使うのか？──それがいわゆるタイプライターのような働きをしてくれるからである。誰がキーを叩いても、所要時間の差こそあれ、一様にきれいにわかりやすく見えるという利点は、不特定多数を相手にするプレゼンテーションにふさわしい。能書家の筆致の味わいには欠けるが、能書は往々にして判読しづらいというのも事実である。これと同じように、上手と下手の差が歴然とする筆塗りに自信のない人でも、丁寧にカットし慎重に吹きつければ、誰の目にも納得できる仕上がりが期待でき、確実に作品の訴求力が増すのである。だからタイプ初心者の一本指打法のように、まずは遅くても面が吹ければよいのであり、しかも、一部分を吹きつけるだけでもパースとして100％の完成度に達することが可能になる。線が本来のパースペクティブであるとすれば、エアブラシングはそれを補完する面の一描法にすぎず、要はその使い方であるからだ。

ただ、筆塗り部分との量的バランスから言えば注意すべき点がある。エアブラシで吹いた面が画面の小さな部分にとどまる程度なら、他の筆塗りの面が目に見えて生きて来る。逆に半分位を占めるようになると、両者の描法の良さは相殺されてしまう。エアブラシした面の硬質で無機物的な光沢と筆の跡に立ち昇るぬくもりとは、あまりに異質である。大気が凪いだ瞬間を写したようなエアブラシの画面に、本然的に暖かさと律動をもった人の筆の運びは介入する余地がない。それどころか後者が妙に稚拙に見えてしまうので、そのような場合は、思いきってエアブラシする面の比率を高めてしまう方がよいだろう。

私がエアブラシを勧めるもう一つの理由は、それが分業化に打ってつけの技法だからである。思う存分時間をかけられるのなら、誰しも自分一人の手で納得のゆく作品を描き上げたい。気持ちのどこかで分業化を潔しとしない人もいるだろう。しかし紛れもなく一個の商品であるパースの制作に流れ作業を導入し、作業効率を高める工夫をすることは当然である。また、分業化が必ずしも複数のチームワークを前提としているわけではない。例えば、一気に筆で描き上げ、塗り上げなければ仕上がりがきれいに出来ない画材や描法がある。このように根気と時間の集中を要する方法に代わって、ペンとインクとエアブラシを用いれば、制作工程が細分化され区切りがつけやすく、作業の中断も自由、複数の作品制作を平行して手際よく進められる。そしてもし「参加することに意義がある」とすれば、初心者でもスタッフの末席に連なり、相応の役割を果たすことが可能なのである。

再び、「イラストレーション・パース」について

副題「エアブラシの展開」からおわかりのように、本書は数年前に出版した拙著「イラストレーション・パースの展開」の続篇である。終始エアブラシに焦点を合わせて編まれた本書だが、末筆にこの変わった表題について再び言及するのは、そこに私のパースに対する考え方が込められているからであり、エアブラシを応用する意図も同じ考え方の延長上に位置付けられるからである。

パースはクライアントを経て、不特定の第三者の視覚に訴えるべく描かれることが多い。いわば卓れて商業的な用途を意識して制作されているにもかかわらず、他の商業グラフィック作品とは一線を画されているように見える。グラフィック作品一般に対して人々が素朴に抱く創作的、象徴的、装飾的なイメージとは無縁に、パースは無人格、没個性の、なるほど「完成予想図」と呼ばれるにふさわしい実用画と見做されがちである。パース自体は確かに作図法に従って機械的に線をなぞれば、一応描き上げられる。しかし、それは単に建築平面図を立体に起こした線の集合にすぎず、見る人に何がしかの印象を残す「絵」としての面白さや、レンダリングとしての図解的な説得力にも欠ける。それなら出来る限りリアルに材質感を表現して、無愛想な線と線の間を埋め尽くし、微細な点まで描出し切ろうと気色ばむと、ますます逆効果になることが多い。少なくとも私は、パースもまた他のグラフィック作品と同様に、形のとらえ方と線と色で決まると思う。より端的に言えば、何事にも共通することだが、描く作業以前の発想や感性で成否の大半は決してしまうのだ。

パースは、何よりもまず設計の意図と対象の形態を明確に伝えると同時に、見る人に実際の空間の広がりを想像させるために在る。しかしこの眼目さえ押さえておけば、レンダラーは自由な裁量で無駄な線や面を整理し、強調すべき部分を緻密に描き込んだりデフォルメするなど工夫して、緩急自在の画面構成を行なうことが許される。またそれが我々の仕事である。つまり、全ての要素を一度吸収した上で美しいものだけを選び出し、それらを改めて過不足なく再構成する一貫したデザイン・プロセスを経て、パースは初めて「絵」になると言える。そしてそのためには、全体の構成だけでなく、パースペクティヴな骨組みに重なる様々な小道具にも、そうしたデザイン的配慮を怠ってはならない。

コンピューターでアッという間に作図が出来上がるこの時代でも、色彩や点景の柔軟な適用・演出は、今のところレンダラーの判断に一任されている。つまり、対象たる建築物を的確に描出した上で、それにいかほどの付加価値を賦与できるかが今日のレンダラーの任務の大半を占めると言っても過言ではない。そしてこうした比重を量れば、パースは「建築物を主題としたイラストレーション」、あるいは「イラストレイティヴ・レンダリング」と考えても良いのではないか？ プレゼンテーションを初めとする各種の応用の現場においても、グラフィック作品一般と変わらぬマテリアルとして、パースに付き物のステレオタイプな処理から脱してもよいのではないだろうか？ 私の「イラストレーション・パース」には、こんな屈折した思いも込められている。

しかしそのためには、レンダラー自身に真先により洗練された感覚や知識や発想が求められる。無意味な装飾過剰や手抜き仕事に等しい、一種のペダンティックな「クリエイター」気取りの仕事ぶりを廃し、自己の中に、図解と意匠のプロとしての美意識に裏付けられた合理的なクラフトマンシップを確立することが肝要であろう。「合理的」とは、プロにとっては無駄を出さないことであり、後進にとっては段階的なレベルアップへの正しい道筋である。完成作品は作者の個性を反映しても作業は出来るだけ単純で効率よく、あるいは、ポイントさえ押さえて工程を踏めば誰でも着実に一歩前進できる、といった経済性重視と平均点志向から私のエアブラシの採用も決められた。余った時間とエネルギーは、技巧以前に大切な感覚の研磨に捧げてほしい。時代の息吹を掴むことが日々の課題なのである。

Airbrushing in Rendering   Eiji Mitooka

There are many books available about airbrushing, both appreciative and practical, advocating the airbrush as an indispensable tool for paintspraying, retouching photographs, rendering of precision machinery and super-realistic art. Too often, architects determine how to use the airbrush on a case by case basis. This results in a trial and error process that often leads to imperfect results.

Although the airbrush is extensively applied to architectural rendering, adding a new dimention to the perspective, the actual condition of applying the airbrush has been somewhat less developed. How to use airbrushing to instill vitality into perspective drawings is the subject of this guide. It provides a general metholology of application that will help you with all types of perspectives. Today, although the airbrush has established itself as the modern medium of the super-realistic, especially in the graphic arts, its origin dates back to the stone ages. In a series of step-by-step drawings with instructions, the book demonstrates the proper airbrushing process. Then it presents a series of drawings that reveal how airbrushing enhances various perspective drawings. You will see how airbrushing is used to highlight trees, roofs, windows, sky, ground, shadows, cars, and people.

Over 200 illustrations — many of them in color — reveal uses of airbrushing on rotring pen drawings, dip pen drawings, pencil drawings, marker pen drawings, .xerox-printed drawings, blue-print drawings, and more. Subjects include houses, townhouses, residential areas, condominiums, resort houses, house and office interiors, museums, cafes, and other structures from many different views. There is also a chapter of drawings of airbrush components, complete with explanations of how the airbrush works and various maintenance procedures.

Thus the question arises — Why the airbrush? The use of the airbrush in perspective work has many advantages, some related to the intrinsic mechanism of the instrument itself and others to its aesthetic quality. Although there is a big difference between the skilled and the unskilled worker in applying paint evenly with a handbrush, even a beginner, if he is careful with the cutting and spraying, can attain remarkable effects with an airbrush. With only a partial application of airbrushing, one can greatly improve the overall condition of the perspective. As an effective complement to handpainted areas, airbrushing should be limited to minor parts. If the airbrushed space occupies about half of the whole surface, its hard and inorganic character becomes incompatible with the warm and human feeling of handpainting, thereby offsetting the merits of both. Another advantage of the airbrush is that it is suitable for the division of labour, so that different members of the staff can work on drawing, cutting, brushing etc. As an efficient and practical value, the concept of working together is indispensable if one wishes to employ airbrushing on perspectives.

This book is a sequel to my first book "Illustration + Perspective". For the moment I would like to delve into the meaning of this title, in order to elucidate my concepts about perspectives in general, and in so doing, to delineate a clear relationship between the use of the airbrush and these concepts. As opposed to the other commercial graphics, which are generically defined with creative, symbolic and decorative images, perspectives are still considered to be anonymous, standardized drawings, realistic and practical in nature. But perspectives of this connotation are no more than a group of lines that have neither the charms of graphic work nor the illustrative intelligibility of rendering. While drawing details as realistically as possible can not generate life into a perspective, the criteria for judging a creative perspective is determined by the way of grasping forms, lines and colours. Perspectives exist to communicate the purpose of the design and to convey a reality of its space. If these points are respected, the renderer is free to eliminate excessive lines, to add scrupulous drawing or to concentrate on the parts to be emphasized. All perspectives, before they become picturesque must go through this design process, in which all the elements are once absorbed and then, after choosing only the valuable elements, are reconstructed. To make an attractive 'picture' you should be careful not only to choose the right angle or composition, but also adequate related elements, that when overlaid on the perspective lines accentuate the general impression.

In this computer age where even rendering plans can be done by machine, we must utilize our full artistic ability to imbue the architecture with creative energy. Considering the importance of these elements, perspectives should be called 'illustrations featuring architecture' or 'illustrative renderings' and be given a more original treatment in presentation and ads, as in the other graphic arts. Thus, out of this concept my 'Illustration + Perspective' was born. In order to achieve such goals, we should acquire a more sophisticated aesthetic sense, versatile imagination and professional knowledge. At the same time, we should develop a 'retional' and 'effective' modern craftmanship. The application of the airbrush is, for me, a method which leads to the reality of those objectives.

CHAPTER
1
BASIC METHOD
基本技法

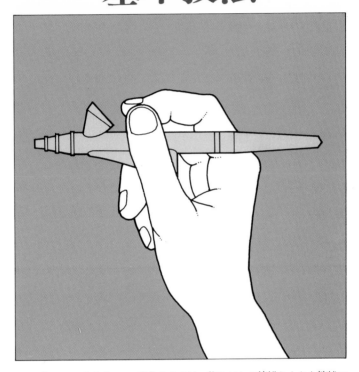

エアブラシングでパースに彩色するのは、往々にして筆描きよりも繁雑に
なることが多いが、基本の手順はあっけないほど単純である。ここでは、
制作プロセスを順を追ってイラストで示し、一葉の住宅パースが完成して
行く段階を辿ってみる。手順以前の問題、即ちエアブラシの操作に欠かせ
ない予備知識や必要な付属器具・画材についての最小の情報は、本書第6章
に簡単にまとめてあるので、初めての人はその章から読んでいただきたい。

Although the colouring of perspectives by airbrushing is often
more complex than that by handpainting, its basic principles
are incredibly simple. In the following pages the developmental
stages required to finish a perspective of a house using the airbrush are demonstrated with step-by-step illustrations of each
process. The preliminary knowledge of operation and the minimum information about its accessories and various media are
presented in chapter 6. Therefore beginners are recommended
to first look at that section before embarking on Chapter 1.

エアブラシングの手順
The Airbrushing Process

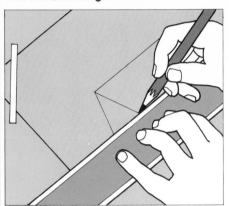

トレシングペーパーに適切な図法によってパースの下描きをし、次に鉛筆で線をなぞりながら正確な輪郭線にまとめる。この時点で点景も描き入れて下描きを完成させる。

With a pencil make clear and precise outlines of the buildings and all related elements represented in the perspective on a sheet of tracing paper, tracing only the necessary lines of the preliminary sketch.

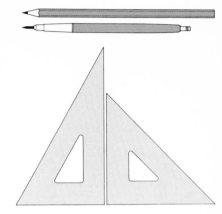

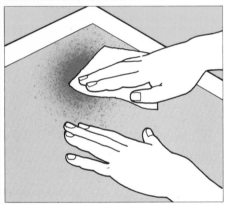

硬く平らな下敷（厚手フィルムなど）の上にトレシングペーパーを裏返し、線が描かれたところ一面に鉛筆の粉（削り器にたまった粉でよい）を柔らかい紙で丁寧にこすりつける。次に厚手のトレシングペーパーで表面をならし、余分な粉ををこすり取る。

On a hard flat sheet (such as a thick plastic film) carefully reverse the tracing paper and rub powdered lead (from the pencil sharpener deposit) over the drawing and around its periphery. Smooth the surface with a sheet of hard tracing paper, rubbing the excess lead powder away.

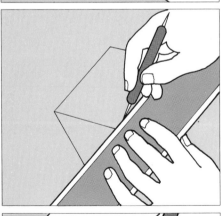

イラストボードの上にトレシングペーパーを置き、四隅の位置を印してテープで留め、特に鋭利な先端の鉄筆でトレースダウンする。細かい曲線部分には鉛筆（6H程度）を使う。ボードに粉が附着しないよう、むやみに画面に触れないこと。

Lay the tracing paper on an adequate illustration board, taping the edges and corners lightly to hold it in position. Then with a pencil, mark the four corners on the board so as to keep a fixed location. Trace the lines with a very sharp pointed metal pen, and for the curved or delicate lines, use a pencil (approx. 6H). In order to prevent the lead powder sticking onto the board, be careful not to touch the surface too often.

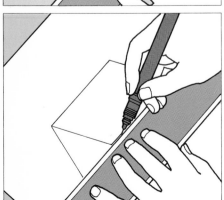

ボードに着いた粉をよくはたき落としてから、トレースした線にロットリングで墨入れをする。この際、各部分のマテリアルに合ったロットリングの太さを選び、随時変えながら完成させる。

After dusting all the lead powder off the board, trace the transferred lines with a Rotring pen. Finish the outlining changing the nib according to the desired effect of each part.

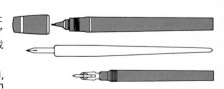

画面の中央から四隅に向かってマスキングフィルムを貼る。この時指先で小刻みに押さえるのではなく、なるべく広い面を使って空気を押し出しながら密着させる。フィルムはボードの寸法と等しくカットするか、小さめに切って周囲を紙で覆う。

Spreading from the center towards the four corners, cover the surface of the board with masking film. Do not try to push it with the fingertips, but, rather spread it with as wide a surface of the hand as possible, simultaneously pushing out the air. When the film covers the area of the board or that a little smaller than the board, cut it and surround it with paper.

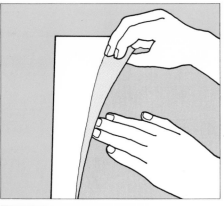

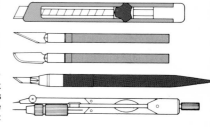

ブラシングする部分の全ての輪郭線をカットする。直線は定規を当ててカッターナイフで切るが、曲線や細かな部分にはスクラッチナイフが扱いやすい。フィルムだけに切り込みを入れるので、スムースに切れるよう常に新しい刃を補充しておく。

Cut into the lines of all those parts designated to be airbrushed. Use a cutter's knife and a scale to cut straight lines, and for cutting curved or delicate lines a scratch knife is easy to handle. Make sure that the blade is new and sharp so that the film will be cut smoothly, leaving the board intact.

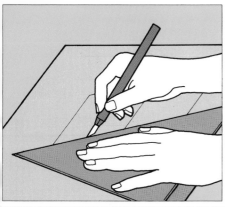

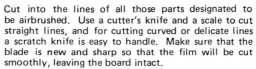

ブラシングの手順を立てて最初に吹く部分をピンセットではがす。普通は、面積が広く形の単純な部分から始める。いったんはがした部分の多くは貼り戻すので、ケント紙などに仮貼りして整理しておく。

Draw up a plan for the airbrushing procedure, sequencing and labelling each process. Then, with a pincette, peel off the part which is supposed to be airbrushed first. Since most of the peeled parts must be re-attached to their original surface, they should be stored safely and categorically It is suggested that they be pasted to another sheet of paper, such as Kent paper.

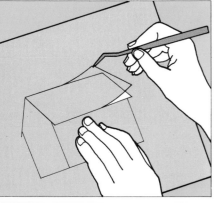

貼がした部分(ここでは屋根)にブラシングする。調合したインクをスポイトでタンクに移し、ハイライトを考えながら吹く。終了すればその部分を貼り戻し、次に吹く部分をはがして同じ手順を操り返す。

Fill the tank with mixed ink using an eye-dropper. Airbrush the previously peeled off part (in this case "roofs") emphasizing the highlighted areas and taking other tonal qualities into consideration. After the airbrushing is finished replace the piece on the surface again. Repeat the same process with the second piece, and so on.

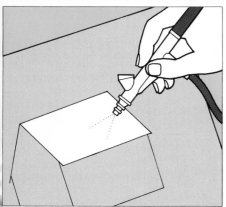

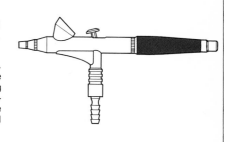

パース制作のプロセス
Developmental Stages of the Perspective

❶

❷

1 鉛筆下描き
2 ロットリング墨入れ
3 エアブラシング──屋根
4 エアブラシング──窓

1 Pencil drawing
2 Outlining in Rotring pen
3 Airbrushed roofs
4 Airbrushed windows

5 エアブラシング──樹木
6 エアブラシング──点景（車、人物）
7 エアブラシング──空、地面
8 エアブラシング──影

5 Airbrushed trees
6 Airbrushed related elements (a car and people)
7 Airbrushed sky and ground
8 Airbrushed shadows

完成パース
Finished Perspective

屋根と空を、グラデーションの方向に気をつけながら、密着マスクを使って吹く。屋根は地面と同様にスパッタリングを施す。

Roofs and the sky are sprayed with contact masking, paying attention to the direction of gradation. Roofs are splattered as well as ground.

住宅の様式や水準に合った車のモデルを選び、建物の邪魔にならない所に配置する。全体の形は密着マスク、ハイライト部分は浮かしマスクで吹く。

Choose an adequate model among various cars according to the style and standard of the house, and put it in a place which does not obstruct the general view of the house. Use contact masking to spray the general form and float masking for the highlights.

人物は家と環境を巡るストーリーを設定する上で、きわめて重要な役割を果たす。要点は丁寧なデッサンと服装の選び方にある。スクラッチナイフでカットし、密着マスクで吹く。

People, being the most effective element in a rendering, can add an articulate dimention to the environment. The key points are to complete a scrupulous sketch and to select the right clothe. Cut out the parts with a scratch knife and spray with contact masking.

樹木は住宅に豊かな雰囲気を与える大切な構成要素である。スクラッチナイフと密着マスクを使って仕上げるが、遠近感をもたせ、ハイライトを引き立たせるために、手前を色濃く表現する。

Trees are considered a constitutional part which provide a house with richness. These parts are cut out with a scratch knife and sprayed with contact masking. Try to make the nearer parts darker in order to give a perspective effect and set the highlights off.

窓は画面全体にメリハリを与えるポイントであり、幅広い色の濃淡、明暗を大胆に使い分ける必要がある。車窓のハイライト部分は浮かしマスク──スリットボーダー──で吹く。

Windows are the most important parts giving a rhythm of tonality to the surface. As they are sprayed both with very dark and light colours, a wide range of light and shadow is required. The highlights of the windows of the car are sprayed with float masking–slit border brushing.

直線的な輪郭をもつ影はカッターナイフで切り、密着マスクを使って吹く。葉の影には、さざめく動きを感じさせる微妙なグラデーションを作り出すよう、スクラッチナイフと浮かしマスクを使う。

Shadows with straight outlines are cut out with a cutter's knife and sprayed with contact masking. Shadows of leaves, on the other hand, are completed with a scratch knife and float masking in order to create a subtle gradation and a realistic impression of the rustling of leaves.

CHAPTER
2
AIRBRUSHING COMPLEMENTING VARIOUS MEDIA
エアブラシと各種 メディア

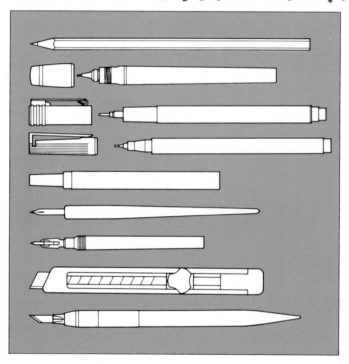

エアブラシングのメディア＝画材＝の選択は、レンダラーの好みや絵の性格によって決まる。章を追って行けばわかるように、私が常用するメディアもほぼ一定している。しかし、ここでは慣用に拘泥らないメディアの組み合わせや、一種の「キット・パース」、あるいは「明るい昼下り」といった定型を無視したパースの試みを紹介したい。中には労多くして益少ない例もあるだろうが、初心者をエアブラシングに誘う縁となれば幸いである。

The preference of the renderer and the characteristic of the perspective are the basic criteria in choosing the media to be used for airbrushing. As is evident in the following pages, I have consistently employed my own favorite media in my perspectives. In this chapter, however, I have attempted to introduce a few uncommon examples: unusual combinations of media, a "kit perspective" and perspectives not related to standard situations, such as, "a house on a sunny afternoon". Although some of them may be impractical because of time and financial factors, I hope these models will generate interest and inspiration for beginners.

エアブラシ＋ロットリング
Airbrushing on Rotring Pen Drawing

A. リゾートハウス外観・玄関部分
B. マンション外観

A. Perspective
   of a Resort House Entrance
B. Exterior Perspective
   of a Condominium

A

B

エアブラシ＋ペン
Airbrushing on Dip Pen Drawing

住宅外観
Exterior Perspective of a House

エアブラシ＋鉛筆
Airbrushing on Pencil Drawing

A.リゾートハウス外観
B.オフィスビル外観

A.Exterior Perspective of a Resort House
B.Exterior Perspective of Office Buildings

A

B

エアブラシ＋フェルトペン
Airbrushing on Marker Pen Drawing

A

A.住宅外観
B.住宅外観

A.Exterior Perspective of a House
B.Exterior Perspective of a House

B

A.住宅インテリア・外観——ロットリング
B.住宅外観——鉛筆

A.Exterior Perspective of a House on the Basis of Rotring Pen Drawing
B.Exterior Perspective of a House on the Basis of Pencil Drawing

エアブラシ＋ゼロックス・コピー
Airbrushing on Xerox-printed Drawing

A

B

エアブラシ＋スクリーントーン
Screentone Film on Airbrushed Parts

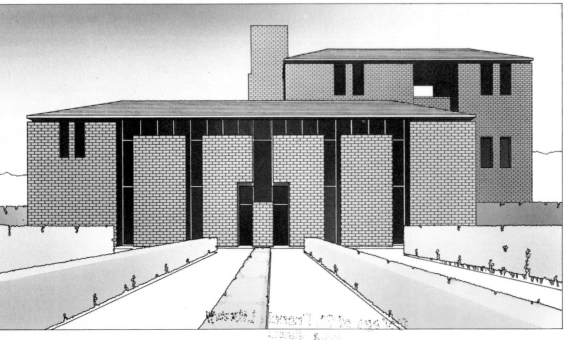

A.住宅インテリア
ブラシングした床と天井部分
に適切なパターンのスクリー
ントーンを貼る
B.学校外観
同様に、壁面をレンガタイル・
パターンで補完する

A. Interior Perspective of a House:
Choose an adequate design among various Screentone film patterns, cut it out and paste it on the previously airbrushed floor and ceiling areas
B. Exterior Perspective of a School:
Brick tile areas are complemented by Screentone film

エアブラシ＋青焼きコピー
Airbrushing on Blue-print Drawing

住宅立面・配置・平面図
Elevation, Site Plan and Plan of a House

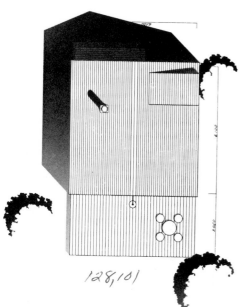

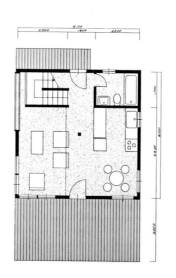

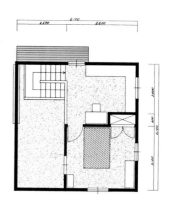

College of St. Francis Library
Joliet, Illinois

エアブラシ＋模型
Airbrushing for Model

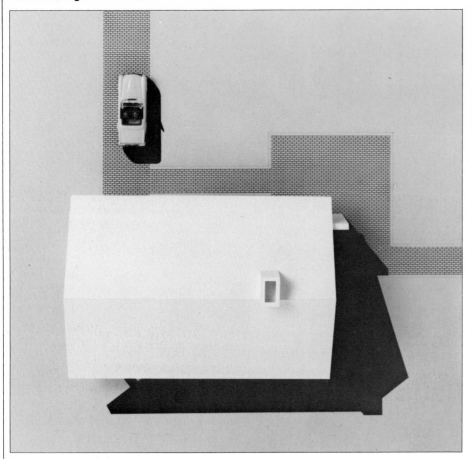

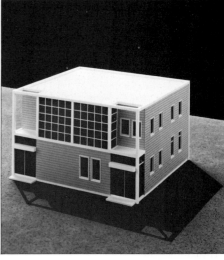

模型を置くボードの表面と建物の影の部分にブラシングする。影の面を付加するだけでも立体感が得られ、建物の形が明確になる。写真に撮れば、絵と模型の中間のような面白いグラフィック効果が生まれる。

Some parts of the model are airbrushed. In addition, shadows on the prepared board are airbrushed in order to give a more realistic impression and to make the outlines clearer. When photographed, a sophisticated graphical effect — between a picture and a model — is produced.

厚手の紙に描いた対象にブラシングしてから
パーツに分解する。ちょうどレリーフ状のキ
ットになり、演出を加えたり背景を変えるこ
とによって様々なプレゼンテーションに利用
できる。

Airbrush on the perspective made
on thick paper then cut into sections. These may form a kind of
versatile relief kit for perspectives
and it could serve as major or
related elements for other presentations if the backgraounds
are changed.

エアブラシ＋「キット・パース」
Airbrushed "Kit Perspective"

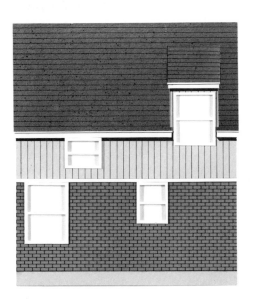

A.樹木、影へのブラシング
B.人物、乗り物、影へのブラシング

A.Airbrushing of Trees and Shadows
B.Airbrushing of a Bicycle, People, Cars and Shadows

部分的エアブラシ
Airbrushing on Specific Areas

A

B

A.日昇──集合住宅外観
B.夜間──住宅外観
余白の窓部分が自と照明効果を上げている

A. Townhouse at Sunrise
B. House in the Night:
Unpainted windows give a lighting effect

時間的差異を表現したエアブラシング
Airbrushing in Various Situations

A

B

各種メディアを使ったエアブラシング
ロットリング、鉛筆、ペン、スパッタリング
**Air brushing on Drawing done
in Rotring Pen, Pencil and by Splattering**

住宅外観
Exterior Perspective of a House

CHAPTER
3
AIRBRUSHING & VARIOUS PERSPECTIVES
エアブラシと各種図法

ここでは、「パース」という名で総称される様々な図法のいくつかを、自作の住宅二棟をモデルに概観する。パースの典型たる一点・二点透視図を省いたのは、平面図や立面図にエアブラシングを一部加えるだけでもプレゼンテーションとして成立することを、実例で示そうと考えたためである。初心者は、カッティングもエアブラシングも簡単な屋根などから試し、あとは丁寧な筆描きのディテールを加えて画面に調子をつけるのが良いだろう。

Using the examples of two houses designed by the author, a general survey of various architectural renderings, generically called perspectives, is presented in the following pages. Because the purpose of this chapter is to demonstrate that even simple plans or elevations can be utilized as a media of perfect presentation with only a partial spray of airbrushing, typical one and two-point drawings of perspectives have been omitted. Initially beginners should airbrush on simple and fixed points, such as roofs, which are easily cut out and peeled off, and complement this with scrupulous handpainting of details and related elements to complete the drawing.

平面図
サイズ ——— A.210×210　B.120×190mm
画材 ——— クレセントボード、ロットリング、カラーインク
ブラシング ——— 床面全体、家具、設備器具

Plans
Size ——— *A. 210 x 210 B. 120 x 190 mm*
Media ——— *Crescent board, Rotring pen and drawing ink*
Airbrushing ——— *Floors, appliances and furniture*

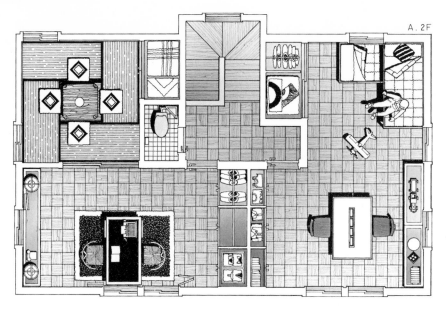

A. 2F

B. 1F

アクソメ
サイズ ——— A.200×230　B.230×235mm
画材 ——— クレセントボード、ロットリング、カラーインク
ブラシング —— 床面全体、家具、設備器具
Axonometrics
Size ——— *A. 200 x 230 B. 230 x 235 mm*
Media ——— *Crescent board, Rotring pen and drawing ink*
Airbrushing —— *Floors, appliances and furniture*

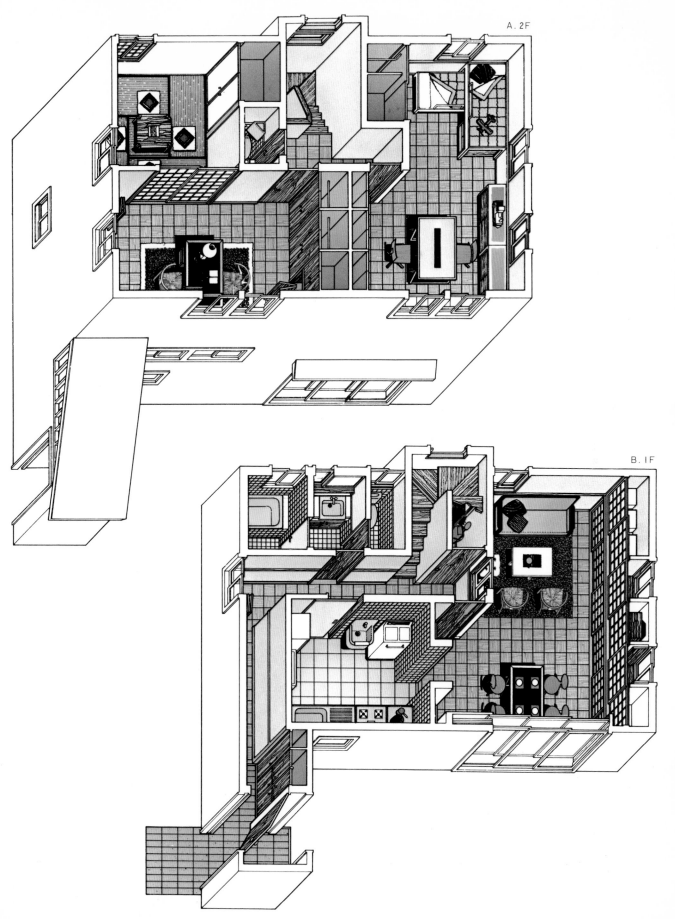

A. 2F

B. 1F

立面図
サイズ ——— A.100×245 B.100×230 C.100×200 D.110×205㎜
画材 ——————— クレセントボード、ロットリング、カラーインク
ブラシング —— 窓、土、影、屋根はスパッタリング

Elevations
Size ————— *A. 100 x 245 B. 110 x 230*
            C. 100 x 200 D. 110 x 205 mm
Media ———— *Crescent board, Rotring pen and drawing ink*
Airbrushing — *Windows, land and shadows. Roofs are splattered*

C

D

配置図
サイズ ——— 230×190mm
画材 ——— クレセントボード、ロットリング、カラーインク
ブラシング —— ベンチ、車、木を除いて全面、屋根はスパッタリング
Site Plan
Size——— 230 x 190 mm
Media——— Crescent board, Rotring pen and drawing ink
Airbrushing— All areas except for benches, a car and trees. Roofs are splattered

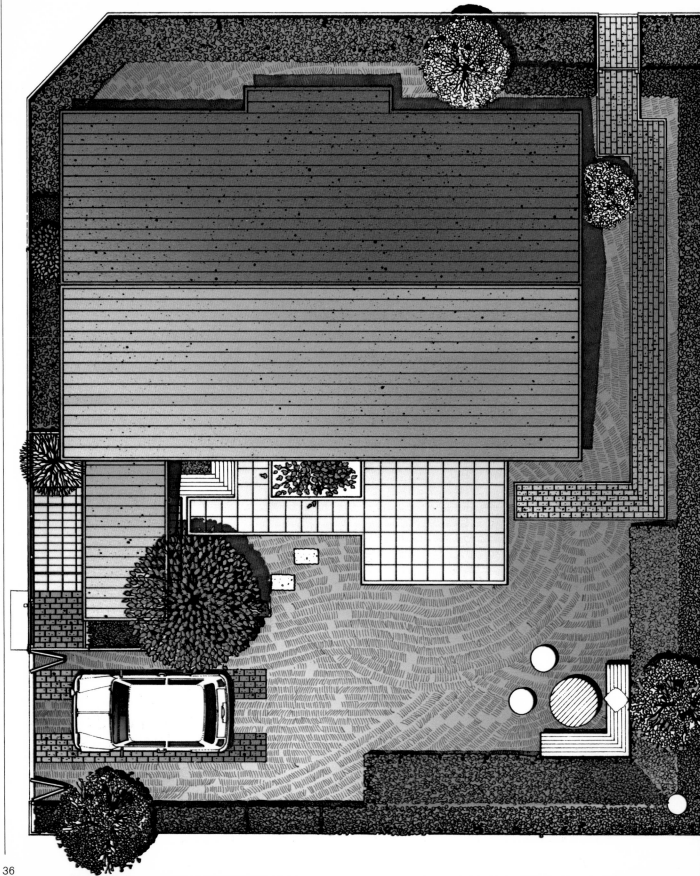

アクソメ
サイズ —————— 250×220mm
画材 ————————— クレセントボード、ロットリング、カラーインク
ブラシング ———— ベンチ、車、木を除いて全面、屋根はスパッタリング
Axonometric
Size————————— 250 x 220 mm
Media————————— Crescent board, Rotring pen and drawing pen
Airbrushing——— All areas except for benches, a car and trees. Roofs are splattered

立面図
サイズ ——— 420×550㎜
画材 ——— クレセントボード、ロットリング、カラーインク
ブラシング ——— 樹木と柵を除いて全面、屋根はスパッタリング
Elevation
Size——— 420 x 550 mm
Media——— Crescent boad, Rotring pen and drawing ink
Airbrushing— All areas except for fences and trees. Roofs are splattered
右頁
アクソメ
サイズ ——— 360×245㎜
画材 ——— クレセントボード、ロットリング、カラーインク
ブラシング ——— 白壁と柵を除いて全面、屋根はスパッタリング
On the right page :
Axonometrics
Size——— 360 x 245 mm
Media——— Crescent board, Rotring pen and drawing ink
Airbrushing— All areas except for fences and white walls. Roofs are splattered

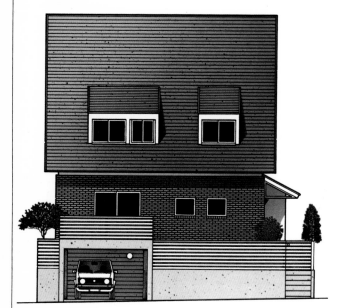

断面図
サイズ ——— 365×630㎜
画材 ——————— クレセントボード、ロットリング、カラーインク
ブラシング ——— 外回り白壁と車を除いて全面、屋根はスパッタリング

General Section
Size ———————— *365 x 630 mm*
Media —————— *Crescent board, Rotrin pen and drawing ink*
Airbrushing — *All areas except for exterior white walls and a car. Roofs are splattered*

CHAPTER
4
USE OF AIRBRUSHING IN RENDERING
作品例

住宅
HOUSES

集合住宅
TOWNHOUSES

住宅と街並み
RESIDENTIAL AREAS

マンション
CONDOMINIUMS

別荘
RESORT HOUSES

住宅・オフィスインテリア
HOUSE AND OFFICE INTERIORS

カフェテラス・カーロット
CAFE AND CARLOT

銀行・市民ホール
BANK AND MUNICIPLE CULTURAL CENTER

美術館・歴史的建築物
MUSEUM AND HISTORICAL ARCHITECTURE

ここに掲載するパースは、オリジナル作品数点を除いて、実際のプレゼン
テーションや広告・カタログ類に使用された作品である。用途の違いによ
って画面や作業進行上の制約は異なるが、エアブラシングについて言えば、
なるべく余白を生かし、かつ黒の線と面で要所を引き締めて、その効果を引
き立たせた。輪郭線は黒と緑を基本色とし、パースの用途や全体の色調に
応じてインクを調合し、色の深みと微妙な変化を引き出すよう心掛けた。

Except for the inclusion of a few original perspectives, this
chapter contains those actually displayed in presentations,
advertisements and brochures. The conditions and difficulties
involved in the drawing and working process varied depending
on the purpose of the perspective. I have tried to emphasize
the use of airbrushing as a complementary and dynamic process
in the overall creative product. Utilizing as much as possible
the unpainted parts, the drawing of black lines and surface parts
and the outlines in basic colours of black and green, I have
attempted to show the complementary effect of airbrushing.
The mixing of various hues of ink must be done according to
the purpose and whole tone of the drawing to produce depth
and delicate changes of colour.

住宅外観
サイズ ——— 350×570mm
画材 ——————— クレセントボード、ロットリング、カラーインク
ブラシング —— 屋根、窓、タイル、芝、樹木のシルエット、影
Exterior Perspective of a House
Size ——————— *350 x 570 mm*
Media ———————— *Crescent board, Rotring pen and drawing ink*
Airbrushing — *Roofs, windows, tiles, lawn, silhouette of leaves and shadows*

住宅外観
サイズ ───── A.230×410 B.200×450㎜
画材 ─────── クレセントボード、ロットリング、カラーインク
ブラシング ── 屋根、壁、窓、影
Exterior Perspectives of Houses
Size──────── *A. 230 x 410 B. 200 x 450 mm*
Media──────── *Crescent board, Rotring pen and drawing ink*
Airbrushing── *Roofs, walls, windows and shadows*

A

B

住宅外観
サイズ ——— A.200×460 B.300×450㎜
画材 ——— クレセントボード、ロットリング、カラーインク
ブラシング —— 白色部分、樹木、生垣を除いて全面
Exterior Perspectives of Houses
Size ——— A. 200 x 460 B. 300 x 450 mm
Media ——— Crescent board, Rotring pen and drawing ink
Airbrushing — All areas except for white parts, trees and hedges

A

B

住宅インテリア
サイズ ——— 370×360mm
画材 ———— クレセントボード、ロットリング、丸ペン、カラーインク
ブラシング —— 床、天井、家具一部
Interior Perspective of a House
Size ———— 370 x 360 mm
Media ———— Crescent board, Rotring pen, dip pen and drawing ink
Airbrushing — Wooden and carpeted floors, ceiling and parts of furniture

住宅インテリア
サイズ ——— 450×480mm
画材 ——— クレセントボード、ロットリング、鉛筆、カラーインク
ブラシング —— 床、天井、小物、空
Interior Perspective of a House
Size ——— *450 x 480 mm*
Media ——— *Crescent board, Rotring pen, pencil and drawing ink*
Airbrushing — *Floors, ceiling, related elements and the sky*

住宅外観
サイズ ——— 265×405mm
画材 ———————— クレセントボード、ロットリング、カラーインク
ブラシング —— 屋根、窓、影
Exterior Perspective of a House
Size——————— 265 x 405 mm
Media————— Crescent board, Rotring pen
Airbrushing— Roofs, windows and shadows

住宅外観
サイズ ——————— A. 210×385 B. 185×500mm
画材 ——————— クレセントボード、ロットリング、丸ペン、カラーインク
ブラシング —————— 屋根、窓、壁面一部、道路、影

Exterior Perspectives of Houses
Size———————— *A. 210 x 385 B. 185 x 500 mm*
Media———————— *Crescent board, Rotring pen, dip pen and drawing ink*
Airbrushing———— *Roofs, windows, parts of walls, streets and shadows*

A

B

住宅と街並み
サイズ ——— 400×740mm
画材 ——————— クレセントボード、ロットリング、カラーインク
ブラシング —— 屋根、窓、道路、影
Perspective of a Residential Area
Size————— 400 x 740 mm
Media ————— Crescent board, Rotring pen and drawing ink
Airbrushing— Roofs, windows, street and shadows

住宅と街並み
サイズ ——— 400×740mm
画材 ——————— クレセントボード、ロットリング、カラーインク
ブラシング —— 屋根、窓、道路、影
Perspective of a Residential Area
Size————— 400 x 740 mm
Media ————— Crescent board, Rotring pen and drawing ink
Airbrushing— Roofs, windows, street and shadows

住宅と街並み
サイズ ——— 300×660mm
画材 ——— クレセントボード、印画紙、ロットリング、カラーインク
ブラシング ——— 屋根、窓、空、影

Perspective of a Residential Area
Size ——— *300 x 660 mm*
Media ——— *Crescent board, Rotring pen and drawing ink.*
In addition, airbrushing and pen drawing were
applied on an enlarged photograph of the
original drawing for the purpose of retouching
Airbrushing — *Roofs, windows, shadows and the sky*

住宅鳥瞰図
サイズ ——— 450×450mm
画材 ——————— クレセントボード、ロットリング、カラーインク
ブラシング —— 屋根、窓、芝、小物、影
Bird's-eye View of a House
Size ——— *450 x 450 mm*
Media ——— *Crescent board, Rotring pen and drawing ink*
Airbrushing — *Roofs, lawn, windows, shadows and related elements*

ユニット住宅外観
サイズ ——— 400×450mm
画材 ——————— クレセントボード、ロットリング、カラーインク
ブラシング —— 窓、芝、影
Exterior Perspective of a Modular House
Size —————— *400 x 450 mm*
Media ————— *Crescent board, Rotring pen and drawing ink*
Airbrushing— *Windows, lawn and shadows*

住宅断面図
サイズ ——— 360×570mm
画材 ——— クレセントボード、ロットリング、カラーインク
ブラシング —— 車、家具、設備器具、小物
General Section of a House
Size ——— 360 x 570 mm
Media ——— Crescent board, Rotring pen and drawing ink
Airbrushing — Furniture, a car, appliances and related elements

マンション立面・外観
サイズ ——— A.120×520　B.230×550㎜
画材 ——— クレセントボード、ロットリング、カラーインク
ブラシング —— 車、人物、樹木を除いて全面、レンガタイルは筆描き併用
Elevation and Exterior Perspective of Condominiums
Size ——— *A. 120 x 520 B. 230 x 550 mm*
Media ——— *Crescent board, Rotring pen and drawing ink*
Airbrushing— *All areas except for cars, people and trees.*
Bricktiles are complemented by handpainting

住宅と街並み
サイズ ——— A.185×460 B.160×460 C.160×810㎜
画材 ——— クレセントボード、ロットリング、カラーインク
ブラシング —— 屋根、窓、壁面の一部、道路、車、影
Exterior Perspectives of Houses and Block Housing
Size ——— *A. 185 x 460 B. 160 x 460 C. 160 x 810 mm*
Media ——— *Crescent board, Rotring pen and drawing ink*
Airbrushing — *Roofs, windows, parts of walls, cars, street and shadows*

A

C

街並みの立面・断面図
サイズ ——— A.180×710 B.180×710mm
画材 ——— クレセントボード、ロットリング、カラーインク
ブラシング —— 窓、小物
Elevation and Sections of a Street Scene
Size ——— A. 180 x 710 B. 180 x 710 mm
Media ——— Crescent board, Rotring pen and drawing ink
Airbrushing — Windows and related elements

A

B

住宅断面図
サイズ ——————— 180×840㎜
画材 ——————— クレセントボード、ロットリング、カラーインク
ブラシング —————— 家具、設備器具、人物、小物
General Section of a House
Size —————— 180 x 840 mm
Media —————— Crescent board, Rotring pen and drawing ink
Airbrushing— Furniture, appliances, people and related elements

オフイスインテリア
サイズ ─────── A.460×420　B.460×550㎜
画材 ─────── クレセントボード、ロットリング、カラーインク
ブラシング ── 白色部分を除いて全面
Isometric and Perspective of Office Interiors
Size ─────── *A.460 x 420 B.460 x 550 mm*
Media ─────── *Crescent board, Rotring pen and drawing ink*
Airbrushing ─── *All areas except for white parts*

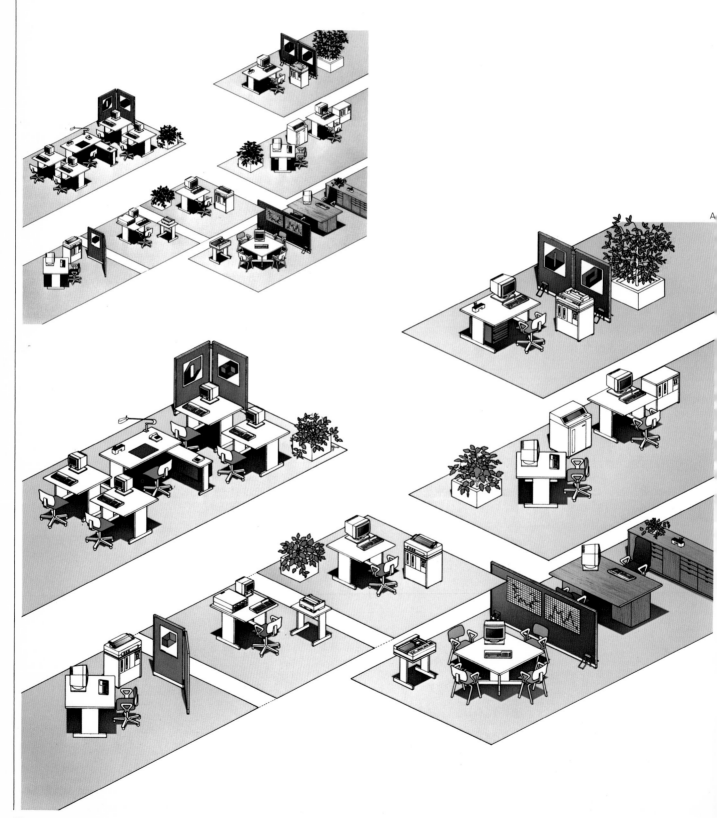

オフイスインテリア
サイズ ─────── A.460×420　B.460×550㎜
画材 ─────── クレセントボード、ロットリング、カラーインク
ブラシング ── 白色部分を除いて全面
Isometric and Perspective of Office Interiors
Size ─────── *A.460 x 420 B.460 x 550 mm*
Media ─────── *Crescent board, Rotring pen and drawing ink*
Airbrushing ─── *All areas except for white parts*

次頁
カフェテラス・中庭
サイズ ─────── 380×525mm
画材 ─────── クレセントボード、ロットリング、カラーインク
ブラシング ──── 窓、芝、レンガ、葉は一部スパッタリング

On the following page :
Perspective of a Cafe Courtyard
Size ─────── 380 x 525 mm
Media ────── Crescent board, Rotring pen and drawing ink
Airbrushing ── Windows, lawn, bricks and leaves. Parts of leaves are splattered

カーロット外観・断面・平面図
サイズ ───── A.410×370　B.110×470　C.325×465mm
画材 ─────── クレセントボード、ロットリング、カラーインク
ブラシング ── 白色部分、人物、樹木を除いて全面、アスファルト地面
　　　　　　　　はスパッタリング

Perspective, Section and Plan of a Car lot
Size ─────── A. 410 x 370 B. 110 x 470 C. 325 x 465 mm
Media ───── Crescent board, Rotring pen and drawing ink
Airbrushing─ All areas except for white parts, people and trees. Asphalt areas are splattered

A

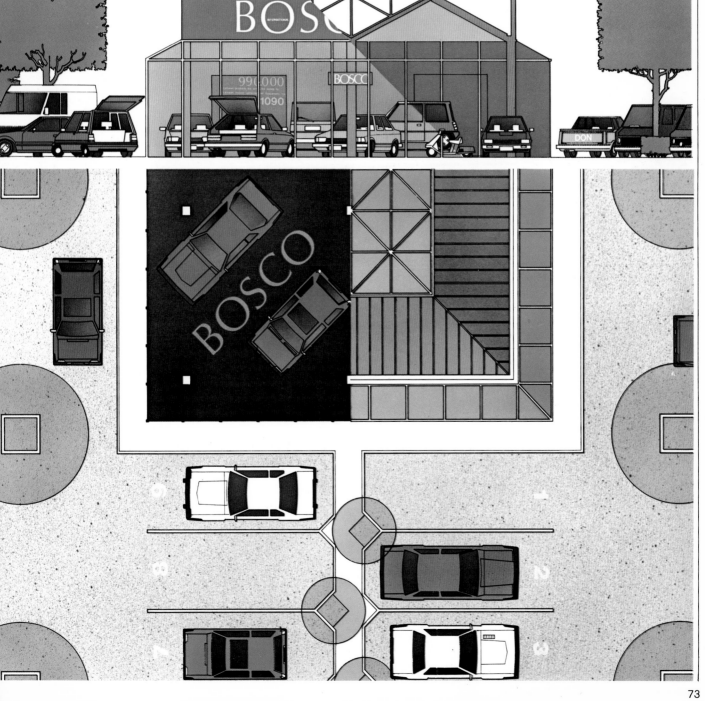

住宅外観
サイズ ——— 330×570㎜
画材 ——— クレセントボード、ロットリング、カラーインク
ブラシング —— 白色部分、人物、樹木一部を除いて全面
House : Exterior Perspective
Size ——— 330 x 570 mm
Media ——— Crescent board, Rotring pen and drawing ink
Airbrushing— All areas except for white parts, people and parts of trees

住宅立面・断面図
サイズ ——— A.220×500　B.175×500　C.175×500　D.420×650㎜
画材 ——— クレセントボード、ロットリング、カラーインク
ブラシング —— 屋根、窓、床、壁、家具、空、影、レンガは筆描き併用
House : Elevations and Perspective Section
Size ——— A. 220 x 500 B. 175 x 500
C. 175 x 500 D. 420 x 650 mm
Media ——— Crescent board, Rotring pen and drawing ink
Airbrushing— Roofs, windows, floors, walls, furniture, shadows and the sky.
Bricks are complemented by handpainting

D

A

B

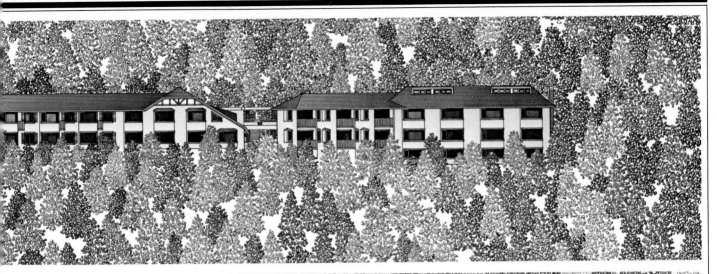

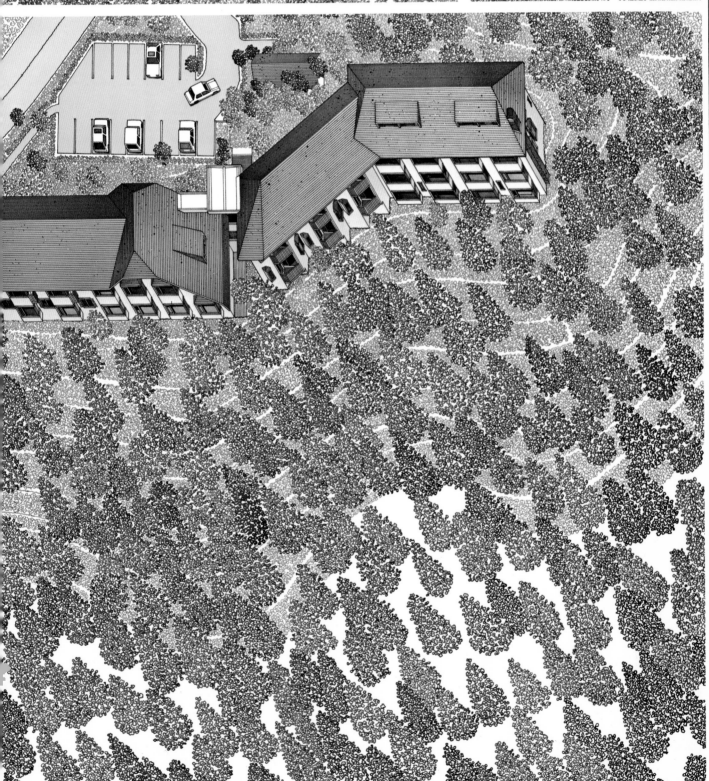

前頁
リゾートマンション立面・鳥瞰図
サイズ ──── A.265×845　B.550×865mm
画材 ──── クレセントボード、ロットリング、カラーインク
ブラシング ── 白色部分と樹木を除いて全面
On the preceeding page :
Elevation and Bird's-eye View of a Resort Condominium
Size ──── *A. 265 x 845 B. 550 x 865 mm*
Media ──── *Crescent board, Rotring pen and drawing ink*
Airbrushing ── *All areas except for white parts and trees*

住宅断面図
サイズ ──── 300×580mm
画材 ──── クレセントボード、ロットリング、カラーインク
ブラシング ── 窓、壁面、家具一部

House : General Section
Size ──── *300 x 580 mm*
Media ──── *Crescent board, Rotring pen and drawing ink*
Airbrushing ── *Windows, walls and parts of furniture*

Elevation and Bird's-eye View of a Resort Condominium

TOKYU 5

住宅外観・平面図
サイズ ────── A.400×580 B.220×200 C.220×280㎜
画材 ────────── クレセントボード、ロットリング、カラーインク
ブラシング ────── 屋根、窓、床、車、家具、影
House : Elevation and Plan
Size ──────── *A. 400 x 580 B. 220 x 200 C. 220 x 280 mm*
Media ──────── *Crescent board, Rotring pen and drawing ink*
Airbrushing── *Roofs, windows, floors, cars, shadows and furniture*

A

B.2F

C.1F

集合住宅断面・外観・鳥瞰図
サイズ ―――― A.360×760　B.370×740　C.380×370mm
画材 ――――― クレセントボード、ロットリング、カラーインク
ブラシング ―― 土、窓、タイル、屋根、樹木一部
Section, Perspective and Birs's-eye View of Townhouses
Size ――――― A. 360 x 760 B. 370 x 740 C. 380 x 370
Media ――――― Crescent board, Rotring pen and drawing ink
Airbrushing ― Land, windows, tiles, roofs and parts of trees

A

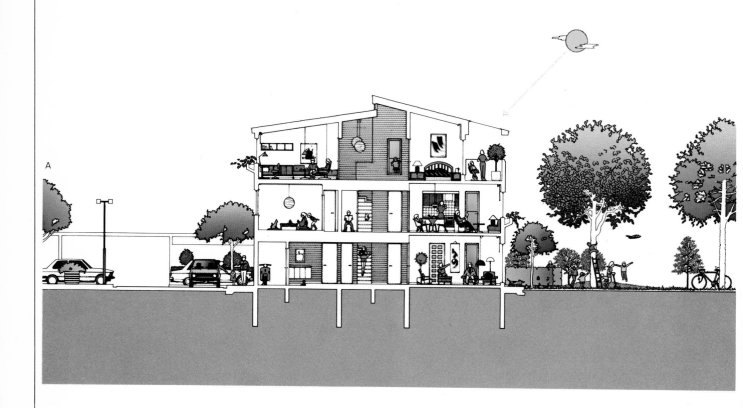

B

リゾートハウス立面図
サイズ ——— 450×810㎜
画材 ——— クレセントボード、ロットリング、カラーインク
ブラシング ——— 白壁と樹木を除いて全面
Resort Houses : Elevation
Size ——— *450 x 810 mm*
Media ——— *Crescent board, Rotring pen and drawing ink*
Airbrushing — *All areas except for white walls and trees*

リゾートハウス・インテリア
サイズ ——— A.360×760　B.370×740　C.380×370㎜
画材 ——— クレセントボード、ロットリング、鉛筆、カラーインク
ブラシング ——— 白色部分、樹木、小物を除いて全面、木部は筆描き併用
Resort Houses : Interior Perspective
Size ——— A. 360 x 760 B. 370 x 740 C. 380 x 370
Media ——— Crescent board, Rotring pen , pencil and drawing ink
Airbrushing — All areas except for white parts, trees and related elements

A

B

C

リゾートハウス鳥瞰図・緑道
サイズ────── A.360×260　B.235×250㎜
画材 ────── クレセントボード、ロットリング、カラーインク
ブラシング ─── 屋根、窓、舗道、木部は筆描き併用
Resort Houses : Partial Bird's-eye View of a House and Footpaths to Houses
Size ────── A. 360 x 260 B. 235 x 250 mm
Media ────── Crescent board, Rotring pen and drawing ink
Airbrushing ─ Roofs, windows and footpaths. Wooden parts are complemented by handpainting

A

B

リゾートハウス鳥瞰図・緑道
サイズ────── A.360×260　B.235×250㎜
画材 ────── クレセントボード、ロットリング、カラーインク
ブラシング ─── 屋根、窓、舗道、木部は筆描き併用
Resort Houses : Partial Bird's-eye View of a House and Footpaths to Houses
Size ────── A. 360 x 260 B. 235 x 250 mm
Media ────── Crescent board, Rotring pen and drawing ink
Airbrushing ─ Roofs, windows and footpaths. Wooden parts are complemented by handpainting

住宅インテリア・鳥瞰
サイズ ——— A.360×360　B.340×310㎜
画材 ——— クレセントボード、ロットリング、カラーインク
ブラシング ——— 白色部分、壁面、樹木、生垣を除いて全面
House : Interior Perspective and Bird's-eye View
Size ——— *A 360 x 360 B. 340 x 310 mm*
Media ——— *Crescent board, Rotring pen and drawing ink*
Airbrushing — *All areas except for white parts, walls, trees and hedges*

A

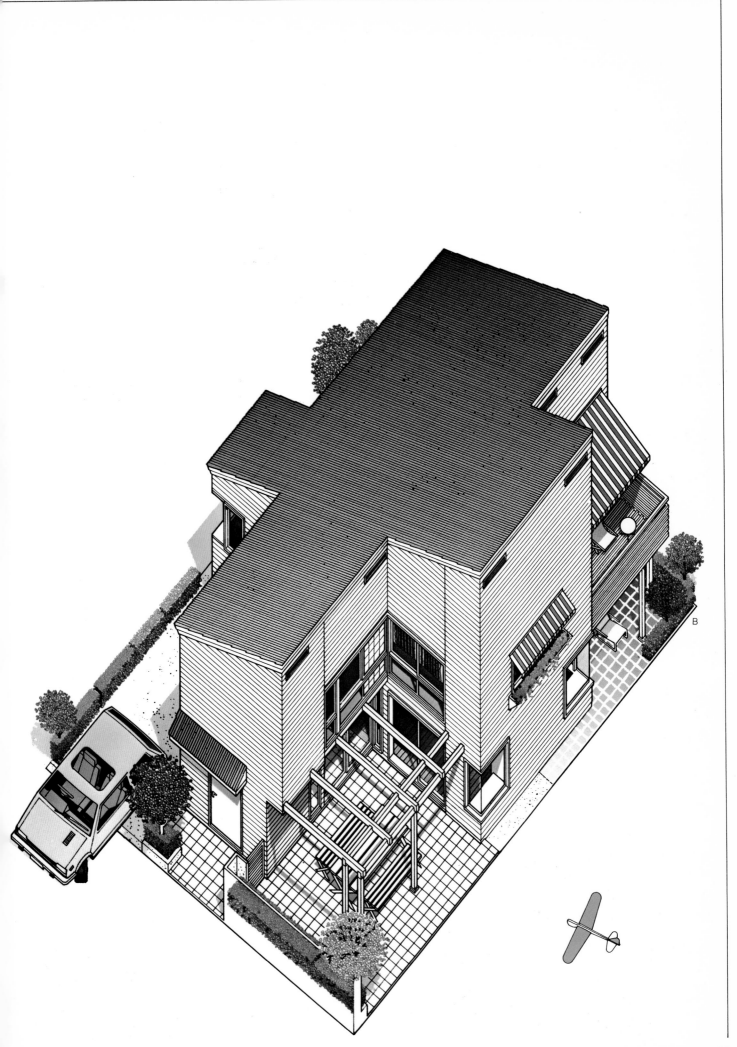

住宅断面図
サイズ ——— A.290×310 B·290×420mm
画材 ——— クレセントボード、ロットリング、カラーインク
ブラシング ——— 屋根、窓、家具、車

House : Sections
Size ——— *A. 290 x 310 B. 290 x 420 mm*
Media ——— *Crescent board, Rotring pen and drawing ink*
Airbrushing — *Roofs, windows, furniture and a car*

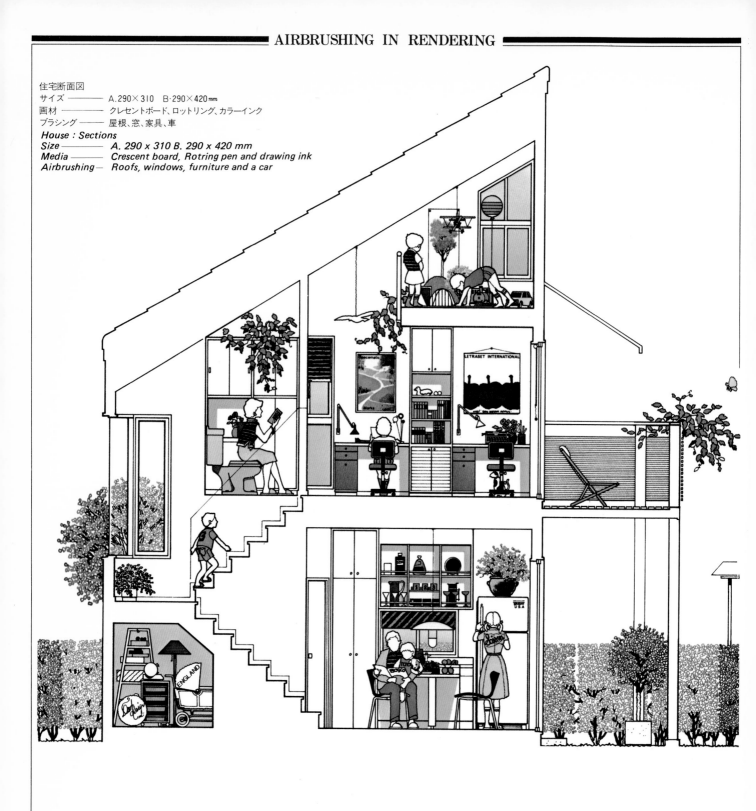

TOILET

BATH

住宅外観
サイズ————460×670mm
画材————クレセントボード、ロットリング、カラーインク
ブラシング——白色部分、芝、樹木を除いて全面

House : Exterior Perspective
Size ———— 460 x 670 mm
Media ———— Crescent board, Rotring pen and drawing ink
Airbrushing — All areas except for white parts, lawn and trees

住宅断面図
サイズ ——— A. 380×1,300　B. 430×730㎜
画材 ——— クレセントボード、ロットリング、カラーインク
ブラシング ——— 白色部分、人物、樹木を除いて全面
House : Sections
Size ——— *A. 380 x 1,300 B. 430 x 730 mm*
Media ——— *Crescent board, Rotring pen and drawing ink*
Airbrushing — *All areas except for white parts, people and trees*

A

B

住宅インテリア
サイズ ——————— A.365×500　B.300×300　C.300×560㎜
画材 ——————— クレセントボード、ロットリング、カラーインク
ブラシング ——— 白色部分、人物、植物、除いて全面、模型では背景と芝.
House : Interior Perspectives
Size —————— *A. 365 x 500 B. 300 x 300 C. 300 x 560 mm*
Media ———— *Crescent board, Rotring pen and drawing ink*
Airbrushing— *All areas except for white parts, people and plants.*
For the model, background and lawn are airbrushed

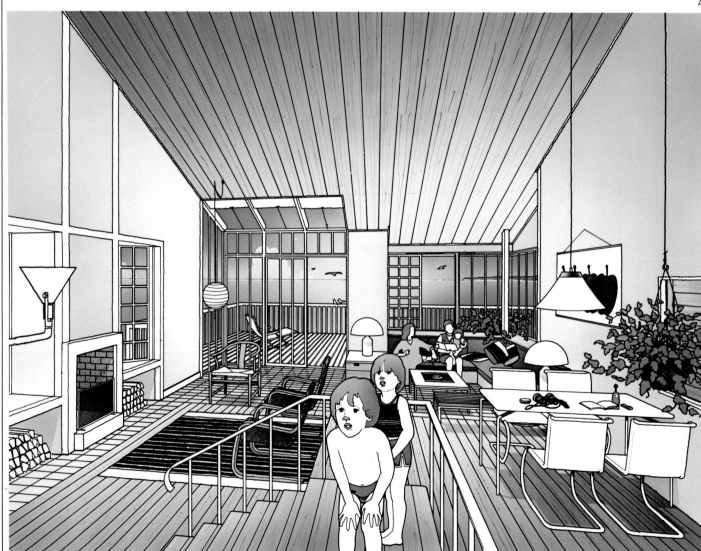

住宅立面図
サイズ ——— 300×560mm
画材 ——— クレセントボード、鉛筆、カラーインク
ブラシング —— 白色部分を除いて全面
House : Elevations
Size ——— *300 x 560 mm*
Media ——— *Crescent board, pencil and drawing ink*
Airbrushing — *All areas except for white parts*

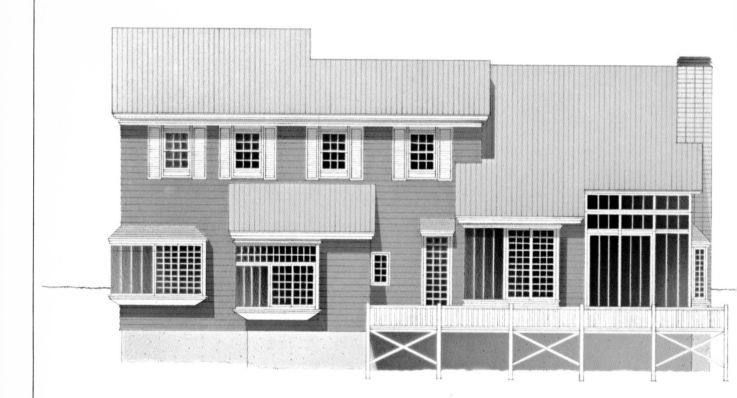

住宅立面図
サイズ ——— 300×560mm
画材 ——— クレセントボード、鉛筆、カラーインク
ブラシング —— 白色部分を除いて全面
House : Elevations
Size ——— *300 x 560 mm*
Media ——— *Crescent board, pencil and drawing ink*
Airbrushing — *All areas except for white parts*

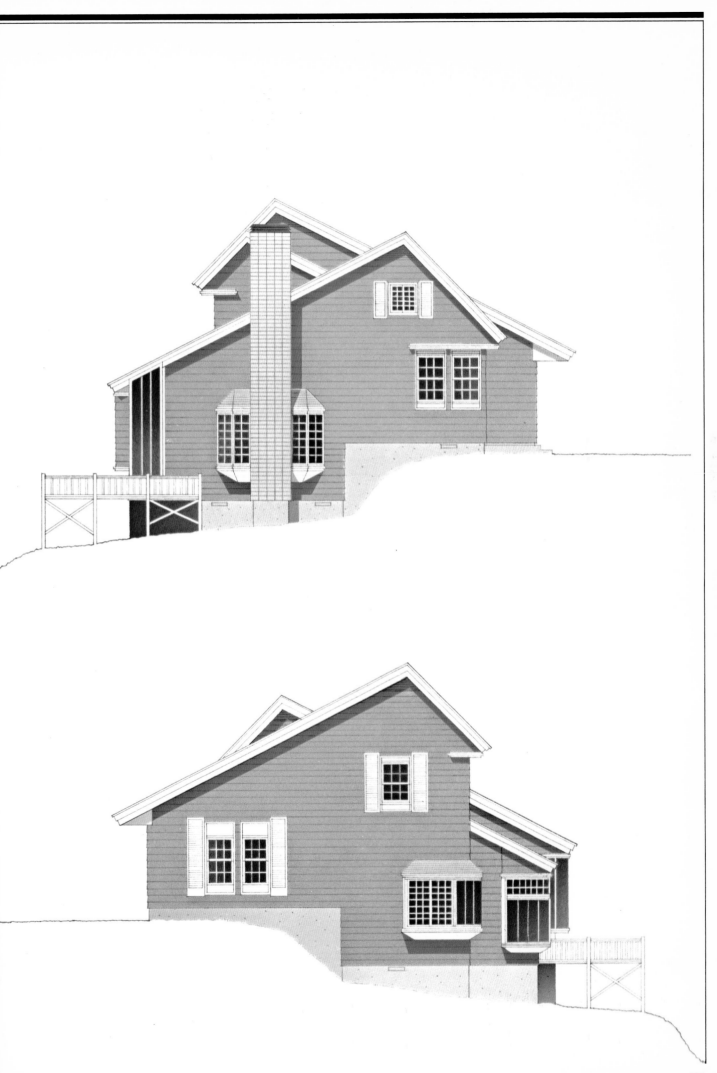

ホテル・ロビーのインテリア
サイズ ——————— 390×360㎜
画材 ——————— クレセントボード、ロットリング、カラーインク
ブラシング —————— 滝、樹木、人物を除いて全面
Interior Perspective of Hotel Foyer
Size ——————— 390 x 360 mm
Media ——————— Crescent board, Rotring pen and drawing ink
Airbrushing — All areas except for water fall, trees and people

銀行外観(スリランカ)
サイズ ——— 500×400㎜
画材 ——— クレセントボード、ロットリング、カラーインク
ブラシング ——— 外壁
Exterior perspective of a Bank in SriLanka
Size ——— 500 x 400 mm
Media ——— Crescent board, Rotring pen and drawing ink
Airbrushing— Exterior walls

次頁
グッゲンハイム美術館外観
サイズ ——— 345×435㎜
画材 ——— クレセントボード、鉛筆、カラーインク
ブラシング ——— 白色部分、樹木、小物を除いて全面
Exterior Perspective of the Solomon R. Guggenheim Museum
Size ——— 345 x 435 mm
Media ——— Crescent board, pencil and drawing ink
Airbrushing — All areas except for·white parts, trees and related elements

日本銀行小樽支店立面図
サイズ ──── 200×345mm
画材 ──── クレセントボード、鉛筆、ロットリング、カラーインク
ブラシング ── 白色部分を除いて全面
Elevation of the Bank of Japan, Otaru Branch
Size ──────── *200 x 345 mm*
Media ──────── *Crescent board, pencil, Rotring pen and drawing ink*
Airbrushing ── *All areas except for white parts*

桂離宮立面図
サイズ ——— 280×700mm
画材 ——— クレセントボード、鉛筆、ロットリング、カラーインク
ブラシング ——— 白色部分を除いて全面
Elevation of the "Katsura–Rikyu" Imperial Villa
Size ——— *280 x 700 mm*
Media ——— *Crescent board, pencil, Rotring pen and drawing ink*
Airbrushing — *All areas except for white parts*

Southeast elevation

Southwest elevation

熊本県立劇場
サイズ —————— 500×700 mm
画材 —————— クレセントボード、ロットリング、カラーインク
ブラシング —————— 白色部分、樹木、人物を除いて全面
Perspective of the Kumamoto Municiple Cultural Center
Size ————— 500 x 700 mm
Media ————— Crescent board, Rotring pen and drawing ink
Airbrushing — All areas except for white parts, trees and people

住宅外観・インテリア
サイズ ─────── A.295×310　B.260×380㎜
画材 ───────── クレセントボード、鉛筆、ロットリング、カラーインク
ブラシング ──── 白色部分、樹木を除いて全面
Exterior and Interior Perspectives of a House
Size ─────── A. 295 x 310 B. 260 x 380 mm
Media ─────── Crescent board, pencil, Rotring pen and drawing ink
Airbrushing ── All areas except for white parts and trees

A

B

聴秋閣外観(三溪園)
サイズ ——— 320×300㎜
画材 ——— クレセントボード、鉛筆、ロットリング、カラーインク
ブラシング ——— 白色部分を除いて全面

Exterior Perspective of the "Chosyu-Kaku" Tea House in the "Sankeien" Garden
Size ——— 320 x 300 mm
Media ——— Crescent board, pencil, Rotring pen and drawing ink
Airbrushing — All areas except for white parts

CHAPTER
5
GRAPHIC STUDY OF PERSPECTIVES
USED IN ADVERTISEMENTS

広告創作例

広告素材としてのパースは、もっぱら住宅産業を中心に利用されているが、ここではそれ以外の部門の広告への応用も試みた。グラフィック・デザイナーとレンダラーとの創意の交換が乏しく、双方が月並みな処理に甘んじている現状への自戒を込めて、エアブラシングの視覚的効果と個性の活用を意識した広告の習作を披露する。使用したパースは前章から援用した未発表の作品であり、それに付帯した団体名・企業名は全て架空のものである。

The perspectives in this chapter, although analogous to those displayed in the advertisement of house construction, are concentrated on cafe, office interiors and historical architecture. Furthermore, there are some basic variances of design principles. At present, because of the dichotomy between renderers and graphic designers in the creation of the typical perspective shown in advertisements, there seems to be a negation of the visual elements of colour and dynamic design. A more integrated working relationship between the renderers and graphic designers could produce a much more attractive perspective. In order to instill authenticity, the perspectives and advertisements in this chapter have been created in a realistic fashion. The perspectives came from the author's imagination and the names used in the advertisements bear no relationship to actual organizations or companies.

Newspaper Advertisement

かけがえのない文化遺産を大切に。

明治の人って、開化けてました。凝ってました。

開国によってもたらされた「住」の一大変化は、まず公共の建物に現われた。気鋭の建築家たちが、伝来の知識と洋行体験を妥協で薄めることなく、新生の地に注ぎ込むことが出来た。明治も終ろうとする頃、日本銀行小樽支店が建てられる。長野宇平治の軽快な骨組の上に、辰野金吾の意匠を偲ばせる銅葺きの屋根。それは辰野ルネサンスと呼ぶにふさわしく華麗である。岡田信一郎は、様式の鬼才と謳われたとおり、漸新な破格を試みた。近代の暁鐘を鳴らした時代の気運と誇りは、日本の到る処に、今もひっそりと息づいている。

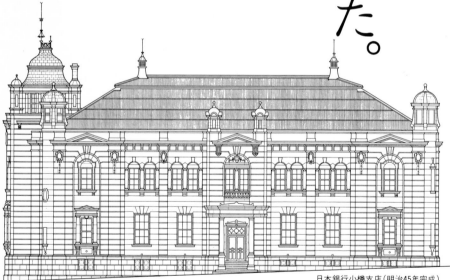

日本銀行小樽支店（明治45年完成）

建築遺産を保存する会
save our architectural heritage

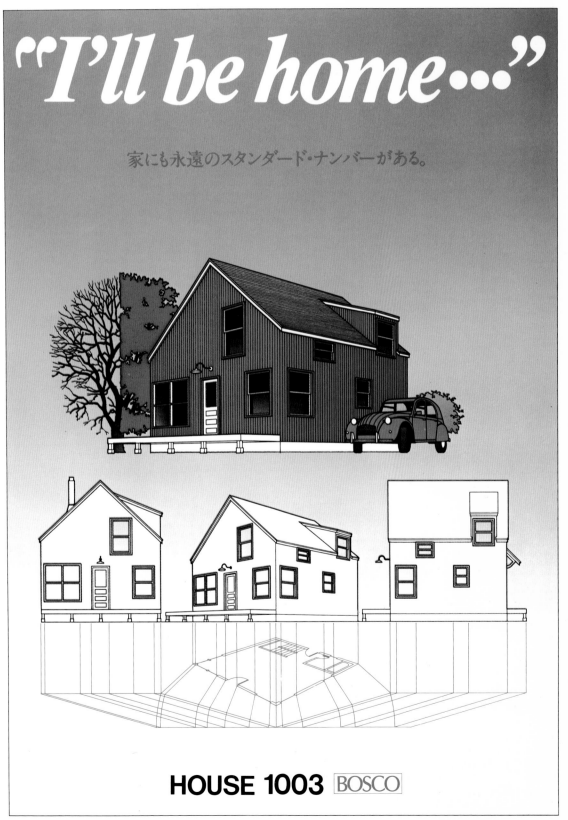

Poster
House designed by
Jeffrey Milstein

Cafe B ある日の午餐 O かすかな葉音 S 木洩れ日やさしく C ティー・フォー・トゥー C

Vivid colours make your office bright!

ヴィヴィッド・カラーはオフィスの頭脳を刺激します。

BOSCO **office furniture & machines**

Poster
House designed by
Hisakazu Harada

"Green, green grass of home…"

家にも永遠のスタンダード・ナンバーがある。

HOUSE 1004 BOSCO

CHAPTER

6

ANATOMY OF THE AIRBRUSH

エアブラシの構造と用具

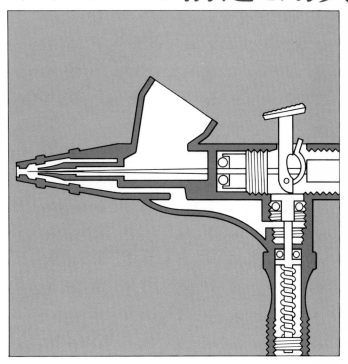

この章には、エアブラシの仕組みと原理から操作や保全の要領、マスキングの仕方、吹き方のＡＢＣまでを簡略に示した。全て、エアブラシの製造・販売メーカーや文具専門店の協力を得て寄せられた情報を集約して編まれたものである。エアブラシの構造や描法を網羅するには、一冊の本を費しても足りぬことだろうが、レンダラーにとって、必要にして最低の技法は限られている。コンパクトな技術マニュアルとして活用していただきたい。

The compilation of this chapter was done with the assistance of the major airbrush manufacturers and stationary shops. In this chapter some fundamental information about the structure and principle of the airbrush, its operation and maintenance, methods of masking and the basic elements of spraying are briefly illustrated. Although to cover all the different structural analyses and ways of drawing using the airbrush would require voluminous content, the minimum and essential techniques for renderers are limited. Therefore, I hope this chapter will be able to serve as a compact technical manual for them.

ハンドピース断面図　Section of the Hand Piece

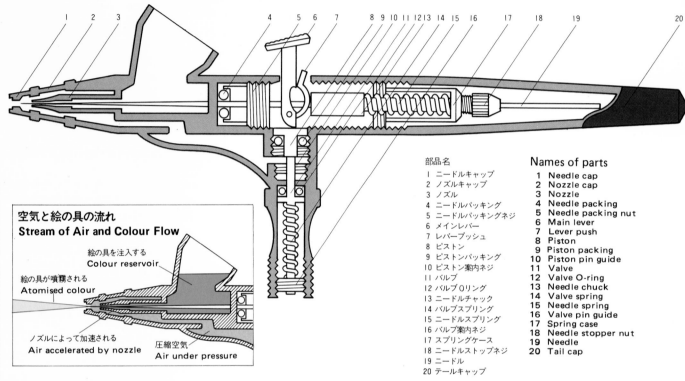

空気と絵の具の流れ
Stream of Air and Colour Flow

絵の具を注入する
Colour reservoir

絵の具が噴霧される
Atomised colour

ノズルによって加速される
Air accelerated by nozzle

圧縮空気
Air under pressure

部品名	Names of parts
1 ニードルキャップ	1 Needle cap
2 ノズルキャップ	2 Nozzle cap
3 ノズル	3 Nozzle
4 ニードルパッキング	4 Needle packing
5 ニードルパッキングネジ	5 Needle packing nut
6 メインレバー	6 Main lever
7 レバーブッシュ	7 Lever push
8 ピストン	8 Piston
9 ピストンパッキング	9 Piston packing
10 ピストン案内ネジ	10 Piston pin guide
11 バルブ	11 Valve
12 バルブOリング	12 Valve O-ring
13 ニードルチャック	13 Needle chuck
14 バルブスプリング	14 Valve spring
15 ニードルスプリング	15 Needle spring
16 バルブ案内ネジ	16 Valve pin guide
17 スプリングケース	17 Spring case
18 ニードルストップネジ	18 Needle stopper nut
19 ニードル	19 Needle
20 テールキャップ	20 Tail cap

This model is manufactured by Olympos Co., Ltd.

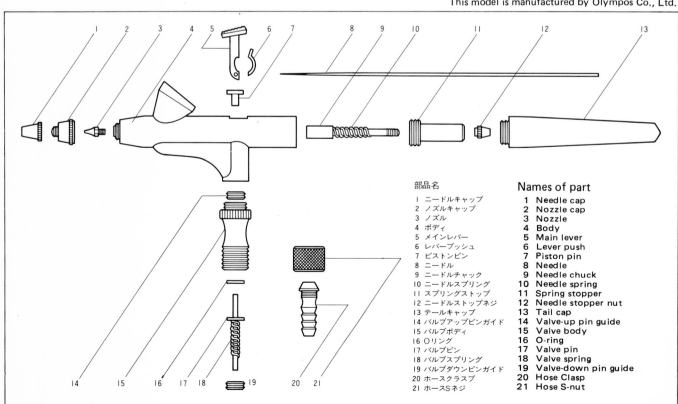

部品名	Names of part
1 ニードルキャップ	1 Needle cap
2 ノズルキャップ	2 Nozzle cap
3 ノズル	3 Nozzle
4 ボディ	4 Body
5 メインレバー	5 Main lever
6 レバーブッシュ	6 Lever push
7 ピストンピン	7 Piston pin
8 ニードル	8 Needle
9 ニードルチャック	9 Needle chuck
10 ニードルスプリング	10 Needle spring
11 スプリングストップ	11 Spring stopper
12 ニードルストップネジ	12 Needle stopper nut
13 テールキャップ	13 Tail cap
14 バルブアップピンガイド	14 Valve-up pin guide
15 バルブボディ	15 Valve body
16 Oリング	16 O-ring
17 バルブピン	17 Valve pin
18 バルブスプリング	18 Valve spring
19 バルブダウンピンガイド	19 Valve-down pin guide
20 ホースクラスプ	20 Hose Clasp
21 ホースSネジ	21 Hose S-nut

ハンドピースの種類　**Types of Hand Piece Products**

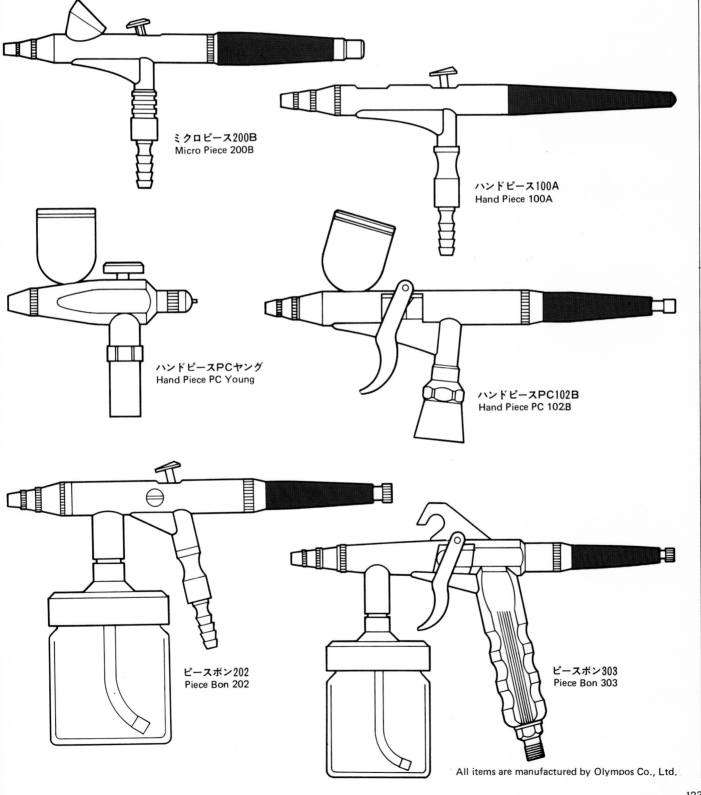

ミクロピース200B
Micro Piece 200B

ハンドピース100A
Hand Piece 100A

ハンドピースPCヤング
Hand Piece PC Young

ハンドピースPC102B
Hand Piece PC 102B

ピースボン202
Piece Bon 202

ピースボン303
Piece Bon 303

All items are manufactured by Olympos Co., Ltd.

コンプレッサーとエアボンベ　Compressor and Disposable Gas Canister

コンプレッサーもエアボンベも、接続されるハンドピースに圧縮空気を送る機能に変わりはないが、使い勝手は大いに異なる。

エアボンベは場所を問わず手軽に使え、音が静かなため、初心者やまれにしか使用しない人には便利である。ただ、長時間続けて使用すると圧力が低下するばかりでなく、ボンベが冷却されて結露するので、本格的にエアブラシを行う人には適さない。

コンプレッサーには多くの器種があるが、出力の大きなものほど安定した空気圧が長時間にわたって得られる。その点、下図の大型コンプレッサー(D、E)が勧められるが、騒音や振動の程度、経済性、設置場所の条件なども考慮して選択すべきである。また、どうしても湿気が排出されるので、清浄器は必ず備えてほしい。

Compressors which provide the air for the hand pieces have been remarkably improved and diversified. They are, of course, operated by motors. As compressors should have a high air pressure they had better large air tanks to keep the pressure at desired point as long as possible. Small, handy-type compressors work rather noiselessly, but cannot keep up the high pressure. Big compressors (D, E), if equipped with an air filter, are highly recommended because they are less noisy, have consistently high pressure and are economical in the long run. Gas canisters can serve as a substitute of compressors and are very convinient because of their compact size and noiselessness, but due to their small capacity they soon cool down and precipitate. The are ideal only for partial spraying and appropriate for beginners.

ダイアフラム式コンプレッサー
（ハンディコンMV1-07S）㈱オリンポス
**Diaphragm Compressor
(Handy Com MV 1—07S) Olympos Co., Ltd.**

リニア式コンプレッサー・中圧用
（A1010-0420）㈱メドー産業
**Linear Compressor for Midium pressure
(A 1010—0420) Medo Sangyo Co., Ltd.**

エアタンク付コンプレッサー（カプセルコン2号）
㈲八重崎鉄工所
**Compressor with Air Tank
(Kapsel-Con No. 2) Yaezaki Tekkosho Inc.**

コンパクト・コンプレッサー
（BA型200W）
㈲八重崎鉄工所
**Compact Compressor (BA 200W)
Yaezaki Tekkosho Inc.**

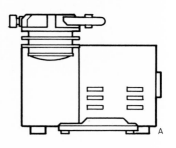

エアタンク付コンプレッサー
（BC-3型）㈲八重崎鉄工所
**Compressor with Air Tank
(BC—3)
Yaezaki Tekkosho Inc.**

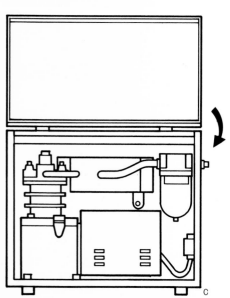

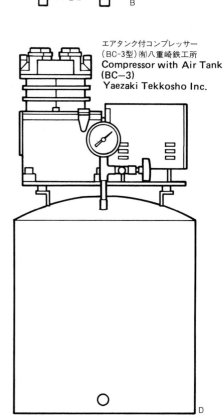

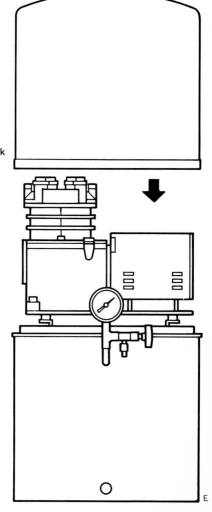

ハンドピースと付属装置の接続　Connection of the Airbrush Equipment to the Hand Piece

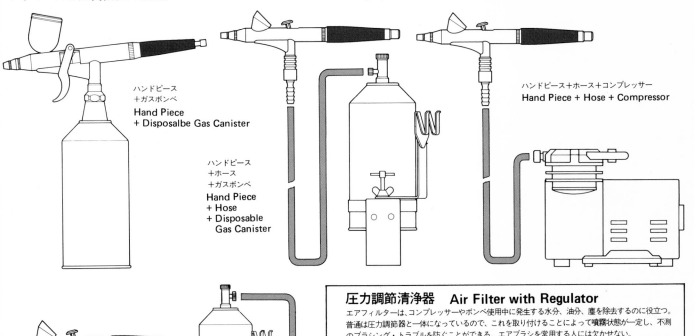

ハンドピース
＋ガスボンベ
Hand Piece
+ Disposalbe Gas Canister

ハンドピース
＋ホース
＋ガスボンベ
Hand Piece
+ Hose
+ Disposable
 Gas Canister

ハンドピース＋ホース＋コンプレッサー
Hand Piece + Hose + Compressor

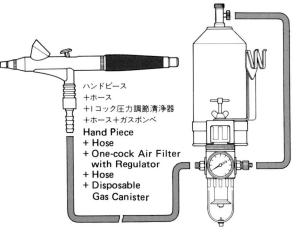

ハンドピース
＋ホース
＋1コック圧力調節清浄器
＋ホース＋ガスボンベ
Hand Piece
+ Hose
+ One-cock Air Filter
 with Regulator
+ Hose
+ Disposable
 Gas Canister

圧力調節清浄器　Air Filter with Regulator

エアフィルターは、コンプレッサーやボンベ使用中に発生する水分、油分、塵を除去するのに役立つ。普通は圧力調節器と一体になっているので、これを取り付けることによって噴霧状態が一定し、不測のブラシング・トラブルを防ぐことができる。エアブラシを常用する人には欠かせない。

The air filter serves to eliminate the excess moisture, oil and dust which are discharged in the air during the operation of the airbrush. It is usually incorporated with a power regulator, and once this equipment is installed the desired effect can be created because of the precisely controlled air pressure. Most of the problems that can arise accidentally may be prevented.

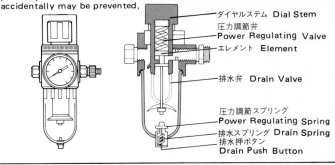

ダイヤルステム　Dial Stem
圧力調節弁　Power Regulating Valve
エレメント　Element

排水弁　Drain Valve

圧力調節スプリング　Power Regulating Spring
排水スプリング　Drain Spring
排水押ボタン　Drain Push Button

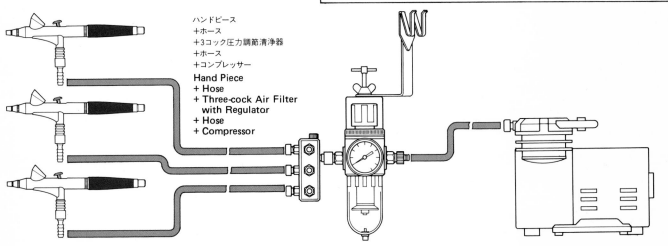

ハンドピース
＋ホース
＋3コック圧力調節清浄器
＋ホース
＋コンプレッサー
Hand Piece
+ Hose
+ Three-cock Air Filter
 with Regulator
+ Hose
+ Compressor

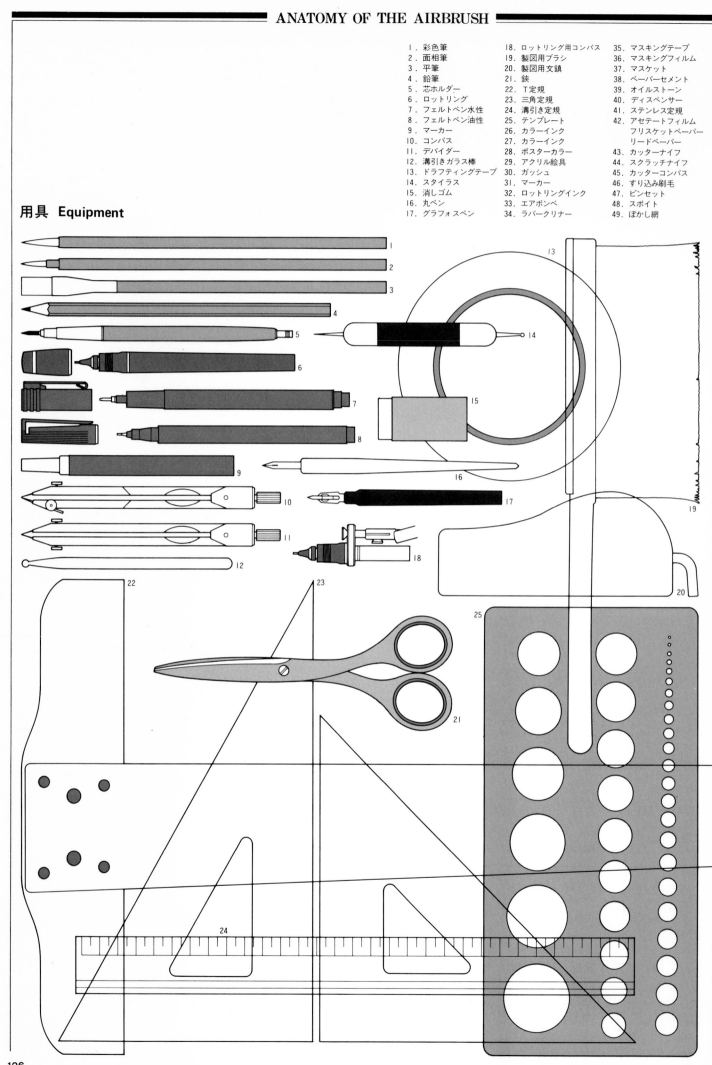

用具 Equipment

1. 彩色筆
2. 面相筆
3. 平筆
4. 鉛筆
5. 芯ホルダー
6. ロットリング
7. フェルトペン水性
8. フェルトペン油性
9. マーカー
10. コンパス
11. デバイダー
12. 溝引きガラス棒
13. ドラフティングテープ
14. スタイラス
15. 消しゴム
16. 丸ペン
17. グラフォスペン
18. ロットリング用コンパス
19. 製図用ブラシ
20. 製図用文鎮
21. 鋏
22. T定規
23. 三角定規
24. 溝引き定規
25. テンプレート
26. カラーインク
27. カラーインク
28. ポスターカラー
29. アクリル絵具
30. ガッシュ
31. マーカー
32. ロットリングインク
33. エアボンベ
34. ラバークリナー
35. マスキングテープ
36. マスキングフィルム
37. マスケット
38. ペーパーセメント
39. オイルストーン
40. ディスペンサー
41. ステンレス定規
42. アセテートフィルム
    フリスケットペーパー
    リードペーパー
43. カッターナイフ
44. スクラッチナイフ
45. カッターコンパス
46. すり込み刷毛
47. ピンセット
48. スポイト
49. ぼかし網

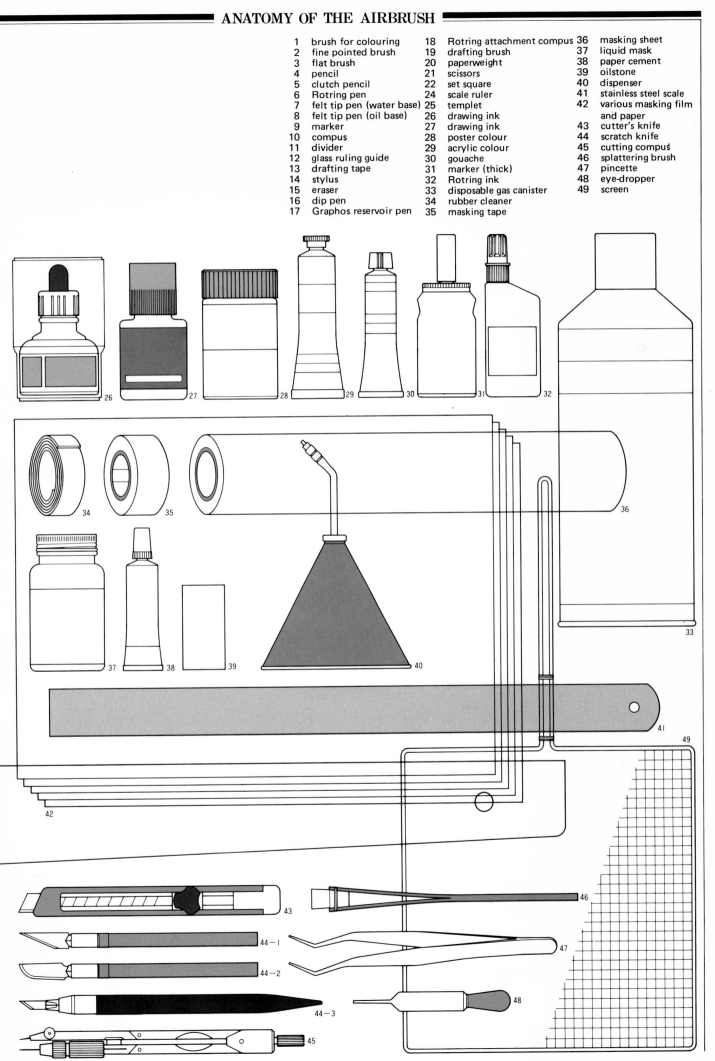

1 brush for colouring
2 fine pointed brush
3 flat brush
4 pencil
5 clutch pencil
6 Rotring pen
7 felt tip pen (water base)
8 felt tip pen (oil base)
9 marker
10 compus
11 divider
12 glass ruling guide
13 drafting tape
14 stylus
15 eraser
16 dip pen
17 Graphos reservoir pen

18 Rotring attachment compus
19 drafting brush
20 paperweight
21 scissors
22 set square
24 scale ruler
25 templet
26 drawing ink
27 drawing ink
28 poster colour
29 acrylic colour
30 gouache
31 marker (thick)
32 Rotring ink
33 disposable gas canister
34 rubber cleaner
35 masking tape

36 masking sheet
37 liquid mask
38 paper cement
39 oilstone
40 dispenser
41 stainless steel scale
42 various masking film
   and paper
43 cutter's knife
44 scratch knife
45 cutting compuś
46 splattering brush
47 pincette
48 eye-dropper
49 screen

エアブラシの操作　Operation of the Airbrush

画面に向かって適切なエアブラシの距離を決め、人差し指でボタンを押して空気を出す。

Holding the hand piece at a fixed distance from the subject matter, press the button with the index finger to release the air.

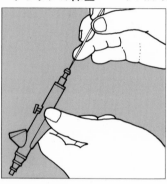

ボタンを手前に引いて絵の具を出す。

To release the colour, pull the button back.

人差し指でボタンを平行に戻し、絵の具の噴射を止める。

To stop the flow of colour, push the button forward to its original position.

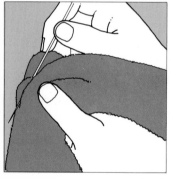

人差し指をボタンから離し、空気を止める。

To stop the flow of air, remove the index finger from the button.

ハンドピースの正しい持ち方 How to hold the hand piece

卵を掌の中に握るようなつもりで持つ

Try to keep the hand as if holding an egg in it.

エアブラシの保全──ノズルの手入れ　Maintenance of the Airbrush ─ Cleaning of the Nozzle

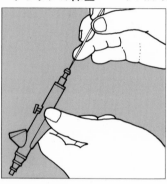

テイルキャップをはずし、ニードルストップねじを緩め、ニードルをゆっくりと取り出す。ノズルキャップを取る。

Remove the tail cap, loosen the needle stopper nut and pull the needle out slowly. Then remove the nozzle cap.

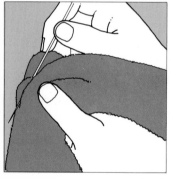

ニードルを曲げないように注意しながら、絵の具や汚れを布で拭き取る。

Wipe off the remaining colour with a cloth. Be careful not bend the needle.

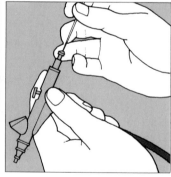

ニードルをゆっくり回しながらハンドピースに差し込む。ニードルの先端が軽くノズルに当たるところで止める。

Insert the needle in the hand piece, rotating the needle slowly until the point touches the nozzle slightly.

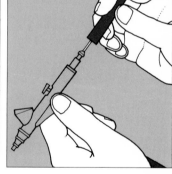

ニードルストップねじを締め、キャップをはめる。

Screw the needle stopper nut, locking it into place, and replace the nozzle cap.

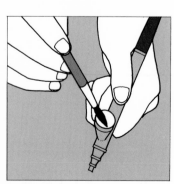

絵の具の交換時はもちろんブラシングの途中でも、時々空気を噴射しながら、水を含ませた筆でタンクの中を洗う。

When changing the colour, release the air and brush the reservoir with a moistened brush to remove the excess colour.

ブラシングが終われば、残った絵の具を全て捨て、空気を噴射しながらタンク内とノズルを水を含ませた細い筆で丁寧に洗う。

After the spraying is finished, remove any remaining colour, release the air and clean the nozzle and reservoir.

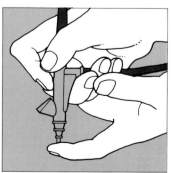

ニードルキャップの先端を指で塞いできれいな水をタンクに入れ、ボタンを押して空気をノズル内に逆流させながら洗浄する。

Close off the end of the needle cap with a finger tip and wash the inside of the reservoir letting the water flow through the nozzle.

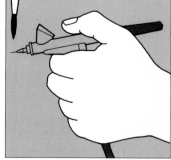

ノズルキャップをはずし、水を含ませた筆の先でノズル周辺を洗う。

Remove the nozzle cap and clean around the nozzle with a brush bristle.

マスキングのいろいろ　Various Masking Methods

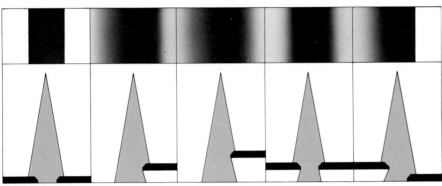

コンタクト——輪郭線を明確に表わすのに欠かせない密着法、建築パースには最も多く利用される

Contact: Indispensable method for creating clear outlines and used most often for architectural rendering.

ロウボーダー——マスクを画面から軽く浮かせて吹くと輪郭線がソフトに仕上がる。利用範囲が広い

Low border: In spraying lift the mask slightly from the paper to make outlines softer. It covers a wide range of usage.

ハイボーダー——マスクを画面から離すほど微妙で滑らかなグラデーションが得られる。背景に利用

High border: The further the airbrush spray the more subtle and smooth gradation is gained. It is often used for backgrounds.

スリットボーダー——隙き間を開けたマスクを通して吹く、メリハリのあるグラデーションが得られる

Slit border: Spray through a slitted mask in order to create a well-contrasted gradation.

シフトボーダー——輪郭線の一方のみをボカす時に使われる、直線が多いパースでは利用頻度が高い

Shift border: Ideal for shading off of one side of the outlines. It is often used in perspectives which have many straight lines.

エアブラシングの距離　Airbrushing Distances from the Surface

距離が大きくなるほどパターンは幅広くなる細い線描は画面から約1cm、狭い面積は約4cm、広い面積は約7cm以上離して吹く、ノズルキャップを取りはずすと砂目模様ができる。

The more distant an airbrush point is, the wider a pattern becomes. With the nozzle cap removed a splattered pattern is created.

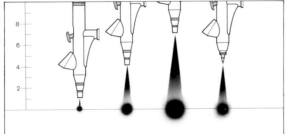

マスケット Liquid Mask

マスケット液を筆で必要な部分に塗る。細い線も自在に描けるので、細密な部分のマスキングに適している。

Apply masking fluid to the desired area with a brush. It is possible to draw fine lines through the fluid.

マスクが乾いたら、画面とエアブラシの距離を適切に定め、必要な部分に吹きつける。

When the mask is dry, spray over the area and the fluid keeping the airbrush at a relative distance above the paper according to the desired effect.

次にインクが完全に乾いたことを確認してから、ゆっくりとこすり取るようにはがす。

To remove the mask rub it gently and peel it off. Be careful to do this only when the colour is perfectly dry.

スパッタリング　Splattering

マスキングフィルムから必要な部分を切り取る。
Cut a mask from plastic film to cover the area which is to be kept clean.

筆に絵の具を含ませる。歯ブラシを使ってもよい。
Dip a brush - a tooth brush will do - in the colour.

平らな表面——厚手フィルムのようなもの——に沿って筆の先を走らせ、絵の具を散らす。
Run the bristle along a straight flat surface - such as thick film - over the area to be splattered.

ぼかし網を使っても、同様の効果が得られる。
Screen surface may be substituted for a straight flat surface.

マスキングフィルムをはがす。
Peel off the masking film.

ブラシングする前に
Preparation Needed Before Airbrushing

換気扇／正しく作動させ、作業場の空気を清浄に保つ。
照明／十分に備え、ブラシングや色の微妙な違いが識別できるようにする。
マスク／絵の具の噴霧から鼻口を保護するために、必ず着用する。
布／吹く前に噴霧の具合を見るのに不可欠。どんな布でもよいが紙は不適。
洗剤／アクリル系インク用に剥離液と洗浄液(固化した時)がある。セラック樹脂系にはメチルアルコールがよい。

Ventilation should be in operating order to keep the air clean in the working space./Lighting should be adequate enough to distinguish the delicate differences of tone, brushing and gradation./Mask is essential to protect the mouth and nose of the operator from the fumes of the spray during airbrushing./Cloths should be available near the working surface in order to allow preliminary testing of the spray before airbrushing on the drawing itself. Floorcloths or waste towels can be used for this purpose, but not paper./Ink remover is very useful in removing acrylic drawing ink, and after it sets, a special strong cleaner is available. For shellac resine drawing ink methyl alcohol is effective.

Index—in Order of Presentation

page · title		type of drawing		size	application
76.	elevation of a house	elevation	B	175×500mm	brochure & poster
	elevation of a house	elevation	C	175×500mm	brochure
77.	Perspective section of a house	one-point perspective	D	420×650mm	brochure
78.	elevation & bird's eye view of a resort condominium	elevation		265×845mm	brochure
	elevation & bird's eye view of a resort condominium	axonometric		550×865mm	brochure
80.	general section of a house	section		410×580mm	brochure & poster
82.	exterior of a house	two-point perspective		300×580mm	brochure & poster
	plan of a house	plan		340×200mm	brochure & poster
84.	general section of townhouses	section	A	360×760mm	competition
	exterior of townhouses	one-point perspective	B	370×740mm	competition
85.	bird's-eye view of townhouses	axonometric	C	380×370mm	competition
86.	exterior of a resort houses	elevation		450×810mm	poster, brochure & leaflet
88.	interior of a resort house:through the window	one-point perspective		240×290mm	brochure & leaflet
89.	interior of a resort house:tatami room	one-point perspective	A	290×380mm	brochure & leaflet
	interior of a resort house dining room	one-point perspective	B	220×260mm	brochure & leaflet
90.	partial view of a resort house	one-point perspective		380×290mm	brochure & leaflet
91.	footpaths to resort houses	one-point perspective		235×250mm	brochure & leaflet
92.	interior of a house	two-point perspective		360×360mm	special pages of a magazine
93.	exterior of a house	axonometric		340×310mm	special pages of a magazine
94.	section of a house	section		290×310mm	special pages of a magazine
95.	section of a house	section		290×500mm	special pages of a magazine
96.	exterior of a resort house	two-point perspective		460×670mm	special pages of a magazine
98.	section of a house	section	A	380×1030mm	special pages of a magazine
	section of a house	section	B	430×730mm	special pages of a magazine
100.	interior of a resort house:living room	two-point perspective	A	365×500mm	special pages of a magazine
101.	interior of a resort house:kitchen	two-point perspective	B	300×300mm	special pages of a magazine
	interior of a resort house:bath room	one-point perspective	C	300×560mm	special pages of a magazine
102.	elevations of a resort house	elevation		300×560mm	
104.	interior of a hotel foyer	three-point perspective		390×360mm	presentation
105.	enterior of a bank	two-point perspective		500×400mm	presentation
106.	exterior of the Guggenheim Museum	two-point perspective		345×435mm	
108.	elevation of the Bank of Japan, Otaru branch	elevation		200×345mm	
110.	elevation of the Katsura-Rikyu imperial villa	elevation		280×700mm	
112.	exterior of the Kumamoto Cultural Center	two-point perspective		500×700mm	presentation
113.	exterior of a house	one-point perspective	A	295×310mm	presentation
	interior of a house	one-point perspective	B	260×380mm	presentation
114.	exterior of the Choshu-Kaku tea house	one-point perspective		320×300mm	

NAGASUE ROKUTAN SHIOJIMA HIROTA   PETER MIURA MITOOKA   SUGAI

SAITO   OHTA

KURODA MURAMOTO

ACKNOWLEDGEMENTS

The author and his associates would like to thank the anonymous readers of his preceeding book published two years ago
and Mr. Michiaki Nagasue of the Graphic-sha Publishing Co.,
Ltd. for their continued support and encouragement.
The author sincerely hopes that this book will provide the
reader with practical ideas as well as aesthetic principles. Rather
than being a complete manual on the art of airbrushing, this
book should serve the purpose of a catalyst to generate ideas
and further exploration.

EIJI MITOOKA

Born in Okayama in 1947.
Graduated from the Industrial Design Course at the Okayama
Industrial High School of Okayama Prefecture.
After having gained experience at the Bizen-kagu Furniture Inc.
in Okayama, the Sun Design Co., Ltd. in Osaka and the Studio
Silvio Coppola in Milan, he founded Don Design Associates Inc.
in Tokyo.
He is a member of the Executive Board of the Japan Archi-
tectural Renderers Association.

あとがき

は「本」に過大な期待を抱いている。今どき犬や猫が本を出しても
も驚かない時勢だろうが、私の本への畏敬の念は変わらない。
が子供の頃、本は楽しいからではなく、タメになるから読むもの
った。だから自分が本を編む身になると、これを読んで下さる方
何か一つタメになることを残したい、と力んでしまう。実益につ
がるヒントでも、「好きな絵もあったな」という仄かな後味でもよ
。それを考える度に筆を投げ出したくなる私を叱咤激励し、出版の運
にまで導いてくれたのは、担当の長末理顕氏と私の処女作を買い
めて下さった読者の方々である。
作スタッフ一同を代表して、ここに心から感謝いたします。

　　　　　　　　　　　　　昭和57年11月　水戸岡鋭治

水戸岡鋭治　　ドーン デザイン研究所代表
　　　　　　　東京都渋谷区神南 1 － 14 － 2
　　　　　　　1947年生　岡山県立岡山工業高校工業デザイン
　　　　　　　科卒　備前家具製作所(岡山)、サン・デザイン
　　　　　　　(大阪)、Studio Silvio Coppola (ミラノ)を経
　　　　　　　て1972年ドーン デザイン研究所設立

スタッフ
レンダリング・アシスタント———菅井茂(兼模型制作)
　　　　　　　　　　　　　　　　六反一光
　　　　　　　　　　　　　　　　弘田雅嗣
　　　　　　　　　　　　　　　　黒田守泰
グラフィック デザイナー————塩島昭彦
　　　　　　　　　　　　　　　　太田克己
エディトリアル・スタッフ————三浦葉子
　　　　　　　　　　　　　　　　ピーター・ヴァン・ゲルダー
制作協力———————————石原繁徳(オリオンフォト)
　　　　　　　　　　　　　　　　斎藤富士男(ばく写真工房)
　　　　　　　　　　　　　　　　ホルベイン工業株式会社
　　　　　　　　　　　　　　　　株式会社 いづみや
　　　　　　　　　　　　　　　　オリンポス株式会社
　　　　　　　　　　　　　　　　有限会社八重崎鉄工所

イラストレーションパース エアブラシの展開
AIRBRUSHING IN RENDERING

著　者　水戸岡鋭治
発行者　富士井 澄
印刷所　錦明印刷株式会社
写　植　有限会社 石井企画
製本所　有限会社 山越製本所
発行所　株式会社 グラフィック社
　　　　〒102 東京都千代田区九段北 1-9-12
　　　　☎ 03(263)4318 振替・東京3-114345

落丁・乱丁はお取り替え致します。

STAFF

Rendering Assistants: Shigeru Sugai (also produced the models)
　　　　　　　　　　Kazumitsu Rokutan
　　　　　　　　　　Masatsugu Hiroṭa
　　　　　　　　　　Moriyasu Kuroda
Graphic Designers　Akihiko Shiojima
　　　　　　　　　　Katsuki Ohta
Editorial Staff　　Yoko Miura
　　　　　　　　　　Peter Van Gelder

The following individuals and manufacturers are thanked for
their invaluable co-operation in the production of this book:
Shigenori Ishihara (Orion Photo Studio), Fujio Saito (Baku
Photo Studio), Holbein Kogyo Co., Ltd., Yaezaki Tekkosho
Inc., Olympos Co., Ltd. Izumiya Co., Ltd.

BIBLIOGRAPHY

Airbrush Illustration Technique (Seibundo Shinko-sha Publish-
ing, Tokyo)
The Airbrush Book (Orbis Publishing, London)
The Complete Guide to Illustration and Design (Phaidon Press
Limited, Oxford)
Abitare No. 174 May 1979 – House displayed on p. 117
Shin Kenchiku July 1982 – Katsura-Rikyu displayed on p. 110
– 111
Jutaku Kenchiku April 1979 – Chosyu-Kaku displayed on p. 114
Architecture and Urbanism July 1981 – Guggenheim Museum
displayed on pp. 106 – 107